The Art and of Directing for Theatre

The formation and communication of vision is one of the primary responsibilities of a director, before ever getting to the nuts and bolts of the process. *The Art and Practice of Directing for Theatre* helps the young director learn how to discover, harness, and meld the two. Providing both a practical and theoretical foundation for directors, this book explores how to craft an artistic vision for a production, and sparks inspiration in directors to put their learning into practice.

This book includes:

- Guidance through day-to-day aspects of directing, including a director's skillset and tools, script analysis, and rehearsal structure.
- Advice on collaborating with production teams and actors, building communication skills and tools, and integrating digital media into these practices.
- Discussion questions and practical worksheets covering script analysis, blocking, and planning rehearsals, with download-able versions on a companion website.

Paul B. Crook is Professor of Theatre at Louisiana Tech University in Ruston, LA, where he teaches both undergraduate and graduate directing and acting courses and supervises all student directing projects, in addition to directing for the Department of Theatre. Paul has previously served as the Director of Theatre Arts for Andrew College in Cuthbert, GA; on the faculty of Shelton State Community College Theatre; as a Distance Educator for the University of Alabama Department of Theatre and Dance; was one of the founding directors of the Kentuck Players in Northport, AL; and also served as the Artistic Coordinator for the SecondStage Theatre in Tuscaloosa, AL.

The Art and Practice of Directing for Theatre

Paul B. Crook

Routledge
Taylor & Francis Group

NEW YORK AND LONDON

First published 2017
by Routledge
711 Third Avenue, New York, NY 10017

and by Routledge
2 Park Square, Milton Park, Abingdon, Oxon OX14 4RN

Routledge is an imprint of the Taylor & Francis Group, an informa business

Library of Congress Cataloging in Publication Data
Names: Crook, Paul B., author.
Title: The art and practice of directing for theatre / Paul B. Crook.
Description: New York : Routledge, 2016. | Includes bibliographical references and index.
Identifiers: LCCN 2016009824| ISBN 9781138948525 (hbk : alk. paper) | ISBN 9781138948518 (pbk : alk. paper) | ISBN 9781315669588 (ebk : alk. paper)
Subjects: LCSH: Theater–Production and direction.
Classification: LCC PN2053 .C76 2016 | DDC 792.02/33–dc23

ISBN: 978-1-138-94852-5 (hbk)
ISBN: 978-1-138-94851-8 (pbk)
ISBN: 978-1-315-66958-8 (ebk)

Typeset in Giovanni Std
by Wearset Ltd, Boldon, Tyne and Wear

Visit the companion website: www.routledge.com/cw/crook

Printed and bound in the United States of America by Sheridan

Contents

Illustrations

Figures

ix

Preface

Why a directing text? Or, more pointedly, why THIS directing text? There are so many wonderful texts available to the student director, what makes this one different? One of the things I have found in my directing classes is that student-directors often have questions about directing that those of us who have been doing it for many years rarely stop to consider any longer. It may be something as basic as "How much attention should I pay to the stage directions in a script?" or it may be something as complex as "How do I integrate the dynamics of the widely varying styles and personalities on my design team?" I find myself spending a great deal of time in class discussing these questions and the results are often quite rewarding and illuminating.

Now, as any directing teacher will tell you, there's no such thing as "A plus B plus C equals directing" (OK, maybe not ANY teacher will tell you that, but it's something I find myself saying an awful lot). The way Granville-Barker did it is not the same way that Guthrie did it and neither is the way that Taymor does it. (Don't recognize those names? Ahhhhhhh! Research and reading are the director's best friends. Look them up! It's OK; I'll wait.)

(Back now? Good.) Every successful director has found a method, a style, and a way to approach a production that works for him or her. Rarely does that translate. When studying directors, it's like walking into one of those huge buffet-style restaurants: you sample a little from this line, then move over to the second line, and then maybe have a little of that sorbet for dessert. You are going to find a style that suits you, and ultimately it will be an amalgam of styles drawn from directors with whom you have worked and learned over the years.

What I've tried to do in putting this text together is offer a basic system of approach that can be expanded upon as you grow, learn, and evolve in your directing life. You can think of this book as the "salad bar" in that huge restaurant. Have a light salad to prepare your director's palate for what you will find as you move from line to line through your career—both educational and, hopefully, professional. By no means is this book meant to be the last word on directing. Hopefully, though, you will find it useful, interesting, and perhaps even entertaining.

Acknowledgments

Writing a textbook is a daunting task, and one that would never have been possible without the assistance of numerous people. First and foremost, thank you to Stacey Walker, with Taylor and Francis. Without your prompting, I never would have even begun this. Also with Taylor and Francis, Meredith Darnell has been fabulous and more helpful than I can ever deserve. Throughout my career, I have been amazingly fortunate to work with some incredible artists. Paul K. Looney, Dr Edmond Williams, and Jonathan Michaelsen were all astounding mentors to me for many years. Whether I was just observing their work or pestering them with questions, they were gracious, open, collaborative, and *wondrously* talented. My colleagues at Louisiana Tech University Department of Theatre, Cherrie Sciro and Mark Guinn, have been more helpful and supportive than anyone could wish. Finally, the wellspring of my inspiration, my wife Mary Fran and our children, George, CeCe, Bryant Ford, and Mary Ellis: I couldn't do *anything* without you. I love you all.

PART I

WHAT IS A DIRECTOR?

CHAPTER 1

Purpose of a Director

Why am I here? No, I'm not talking about the existential mating call version of this question; I'm talking about the question that many directors find themselves faced with upon agreeing to direct a play. For several hundred years, plays were performed (very successfully, I might add) without our help. What changed in the mid-nineteenth century to cause the modern director to be born? Why did dear ol' Georg II, the Duke of Saxe Meiningen feel the need to assert himself? The answer to this one is actually simple and can be expressed in one word: cohesiveness; or vision; or, maybe, unity. OK, that's obviously more than one word, but you get the point.

3

But perhaps that's jumping ahead. In discussing the beginning of her career in the book *A Director Prepares*, Anne Bogart talks about her need to discover "on whose shoulders she stands."[1] Bogart is specifically referring to the importance of examining her "Americanness" as a director, but it is also important to understand how the actual position of director evolved.

From the Greeks forward, there was typically an individual who led a production in some way. Playwrights were most often called upon in the early periods, though some Greek and Roman chorus members also served in that role. Liturgical dramas taking place in European churches in the Middle Ages often had the priest or choirmaster as the individual "in charge." As the popularity of theatre rose again during the Renaissance, we know that Shakespeare, Molière, and a variety of actor-managers assumed the task of leading individual productions. Though few physical records exist, it can even be safely assumed that the patrons of companies sometimes exerted a level of artistic control and vision over performances. We do, of course, have anecdotal evidence from the Melancholy Dane himself: "Speak the speech, I pray you, as I pronounced it to you, trippingly on the tongue; but if you mouth it, as many of your players do, I had as lief the town-crier spoke my lines."[2] From the seventeenth to the nineteenth centuries, any number of people stepped to the fore in "directing" productions, including actors, play-wrights, and theatre owners.

The modern concept of *director*, as an individual whose sole responsibility is to develop and implement a unifying vision for a play, is traditionally traced to 1874 and Georg II, Duke of Saxe-Meiningen. As both the patron and the head of the Meiningen Players, the duke was faced with a lack of funds that forced him to use a team devoid of the star power found in most nineteenth-century acting companies. Faced with this, he chose to focus on finding a cohesion of production that had not previously been seen. In his book *The History of the Theatre*, Oscar Brockett discusses the Meiningen Players' attention to detail in all areas of a production. Brockett notes that Saxe-Meiningen was not only patron and dir-ector, but also served as designer for all the physical elements of his productions. This auteur-like control allowed for a new style of the-atrical production, Brockett tells us: "The impact of the Meiningen Players came from the complete illusion attained in every aspect of the production ... [the company] stands at the beginning of the new movement toward unified production."[3]

So, you see, plays had historically been led by a variety of people: theatre managers, actors, designers, and playwrights all took the helm in various productions, depending on the time and place. If we could jump in the wayback machine, I suspect we would find each of those productions to be glorious displays of disparate parts. What was needed was a person to draw those disparate parts together into a unified whole—hence the birth of the director. So let's bring it back to the present...

Let's say you're directing a production of *King Lear*. You go into your first design meeting and your scenic designer presents you with this glorious PowerPoint production of her vision for the show. She envisions Lear's castle as a beautiful Mayan temple. The castles of his daughters are shown as intricately and ingeniously recreated Mayan dwellings. For the "blasted heath" at the end of the play she has pulled photos and made sketches for a huge cliff from which a waterfall drops into a spectacular lake. Pretty great stuff, right? Really fuels the imagination for a creative, fun version of the show.

Now at that same design meeting, after the scenic designer has presented her ideas, the costume designer (who has grown quieter and quieter during the first presentation) begins his pitch. He has some absolutely amazing sketches and renderings for his costumes. Using plastics and polymers, he has created a stunning, futuristic parade of clothing. He has Lear in a cool space-suit with great lines and a fabulous helmet-crown. Goneril and Regan are in dresses made out of something that looks a little like bubble-wrap, but less fragile. Edgar and Edmund are in diametrically opposed military uniforms of sleek black and white. Finally, the Fool is in a costume that gives him an extra head and three extra limbs.

Now this is just as interesting as the scenic designer's proposal. The problem (aside from the obvious one), though, is that your vision for the show was to place it on Wall Street with Lear as the founding CEO of a technological design firm. So when the costume designer finishes his presentation, you look at both of them and say ... what?

That is why you are there. You possess the ability to take those varying visions and mold them together. You are the ringleader of this 24-ring circus that's called a play. Ultimately, you must remember that the play has to be *your* vision. You have to figure out a way to bring together all of the differing viewpoints of what the play *should* be. It is by no means a simple task and there are certainly many ways to accomplish it, but the successful directors are the ones who find a way to do it. They don't succeed by bludgeoning everyone into doing it their way ... they find a way to show the team how the goal can be accomplished with everyone participating.

Being a director is a lot like being a football coach. A head coach has numerous assistant coaches, each with their own specialty. Each of those coaches is responsible for making sure that a specific section—whether it's the linebackers, the receivers, the quarterbacks, or any other positions—is prepared for each game. The head coach doesn't have to specialize in *all* of those areas, but must have a working knowledge of each area and an overall gameplan, as well as knowing how each person fits into it. Ideally, the offensive, defensive, and special teams coaches are skilled enough that their units are prepared to execute that plan on game day. It might be that, on the sidelines during a crucial point in the game, the running backs

5

coach sidles up to the head coach and says: "Hey, why don't we run slot right, 45 Z-in? I know it will work." The head coach has to make the final decision as to whether that play fits into the overall plan. If it does, the head coach then integrates it into the game but if it doesn't, he or she thanks the assistant coach for the suggestion and then discards it.

The same holds true for you, as a director. You have designers, a technical director, stage management, promotions, etc. Each person wants to produce the best show possible and they all have terrific ideas about how to achieve that goal. You have to listen to their ideas, evaluate how they fit into the overall concept of the show, and decide whether or not to use them. Just remember (and this is jumping ahead to something that will be discussed in a later chapter) that whatever decision you make must be sure to serve the production well. From the first class in theatre you ever took, you have most likely heard that theatre is the most collaborative of all of the arts, and this is true. Within this world of collaboration, though, the director's job is quite possibly the *most* collaborative of them all, since you have to work with everyone in the company to bring the completed vision to the stage for the audience.

So, how do you do all of this? How do you wrangle the circus, coordinate the coaches, assemble all the moving parts? We'll get into specifics throughout the book, but for now let's examine three characteristics of successful directors: passion, vision, and practicality.

Passion

When I talk with classes, or am asked to speak at conferences, or just in conversation with people, I often am asked why I do what I do. My initial answer is always the same, and is only half-joking: I have no other marketable skills! I can't make things; I can't repair things; I'm a horrible salesman; and math makes my head hurt. However, I follow up that somewhat flippant reply with the more pertinent answer, which is this: I have stories to tell. There are hundreds and hundreds of stories out there that I want to share and tell, and directing is my medium to do that. We, directors, are storytellers at heart. And what is so exciting about theatre is that when we tell Nora Helmer's story, or Willy Loman's story, we are really telling *our* story. Every successful director I have ever met or read about has been passionate about telling stories. Directors know that plays are vital expressions of a certain aspect or aspects of society, and through performance we can illuminate those for an audience. The best directors choose plays that they are passionate about and whose stories they feel a driving urge to share with an audience.

Now, obviously, directors aren't going to feel the same level of passion about every play they direct; there are some plays that you simply love more than others. And that's OK. But when faced with a play that isn't as exciting to you as another might be, remember your passion for storytelling. Remember your passion for performances. Remember your passion for theatre. Because the truth is, there will be times you are directing a show that you don't really like at all. Just like every other profession, sometimes we take jobs because we need to have a job. There are bills to pay, food to buy, and families to clothe. This is, perhaps, when your passion is most valuable to you. It's easy to get up and go to work when you jump out of bed and are excited about the prospects of the day—anyone can do that. It gets much more difficult when you're faced with going in to a rehearsal for a play that you don't like or haven't yet been able to get excited about. When that happens, remember your passion: find *something* that excites you about the production. Perhaps it's a particular blocking challenge the play holds, due to the size or shape of the set. Perhaps there's an actor in the show you have always admired but never had the opportunity to work with before. Or perhaps you will get the opportunity to work with a larger budget than you've had on previous shows. Whatever the reason, you have to find a *hook*—something on which you can hang your passion and which will allow you to dive into the play with excitement each day. Because if you aren't able to find that hook, the resulting production will, unfortunately, reflect your lack of passion.

Vision

How do you read a play? Obviously, I'm not asking the question physiologically; I'm asking what you focus on when you read a script. Do you zero in on a particular character? Plot point? Theme? Design? Or do you read it just for entertainment purposes? All of those are certainly valid approaches to reading, but for a director, none of them are complete. Remember that the director is ultimately responsible for providing the vision for the entire production, and you should begin developing that vision at the first reading. Ideally, when you read a script as a director, you should "see" the play unfold in your head in some fashion. While you may have come to directing via some other discipline (acting, design, stage management, etc.), if you only focus on that particular area, then you will miss out on a great deal. If you find yourself focusing on one area while reading a script, then make a conscious effort the next time through to look at the whole picture. We'll be discussing the specifics of approaching a script in a later chapter, but for now a question to bear in mind while reading a script is: What do you want the audience to take away from the performance? Remember that it is *for* the audience that the story is being told, and that each decision you make will impact what the audience gets out of the experience. By keeping this question in your head while reading a play, you will begin to formulate your vision for the overall production.

Sometimes it's hard to figure out where to start in formulating your vision for a show. One way to assist in that process is to consider a show for which you already have a vision. Every director I have ever met has a "Dream Show" in mind. This is a show that, given free rein over decision-making, and an unlimited budget, the director knows exactly how he or she would approach it. Even if you are completely inexperienced, and have taken this class never having considered directing before, you may find that you already have such a show in mind. Remember, the Dream Show isn't logical—you're never going to be given an unlimited budget—but logic doesn't have to matter. You know the show you *want* to do, and you know the *way* you want to do it. Consider what your Dream Show is (or what it might be). Examine the vision you have of the show in your head (concept, design choices, casting, staging, etc.). Take note of how much you know about the show already, before you've even started researching it, and then begin to look for those elements in your new script. By considering the various parts of your vision for your Dream Show, you begin to see everything that needs to be developed to formulate your vision for any script that you read.

Practicality

The Dream Show notwithstanding (remember that logic doesn't matter there), you have to maintain a strong sense of practicality to support the artistry of your vision. By no means does this mean you should stifle creativity, dreaming, or flat-out wishful thinking as an artist, but it does mean that you have to recognize the fact that we, as directors, live in the real world, just like everyone else. There are many aspects to practicality, including show selection, budget, design concept, and casting choices, to name just a few. Have you been hired to direct a show at a church-owned college? Then *Marat/Sade* or *Caligula* probably shouldn't be on your show selection list. Are you performing in a 50-seat black-box theatre? Then you probably won't be able to have a fully realistic set and costumes for *Cyrano de Bergerac*. Are you teaching at an all-boys school? Then you probably shouldn't try and do *The Women*.

Practicality goes hand in hand with vision: think of it as the *ego* to your *id*. Your vision is creative and artistic, but your practicality is realistic. Producers get excited about artistic vision (and the best ones will do everything they can to help you realize your vision), but they deal in the real world of practicality. A director who has a strong sense of both will ultimately be hired and rehired, as producers want to work with directors who are able to maintain a foot in both worlds.

So here we are. The broad brushstrokes describing a director have been set out and now it's time to fill in the details. As we go through the rest of the book, you'll learn how to marry practicality to your artistic vision: the art *and* the practice.

Exercises and Suggested Reading

At the end of each chapter, you will find a list of exercises to allow you to reinforce some of the ideas discussed in the chapter. Also, I will provide you with a suggested reading list, based on books and plays mentioned in the chapter. Some of them may be familiar to you, but for those that are not, pick a few to read, or use the list when you have a choice on a research assignment topic. Remember the preface: "Research and reading are the director's best friends!"

Exercises

1. Choose a director to research. Don't just examine his or her work, but examine who the director is as a person. Look at biographical details, interviews, writings, etc. Report to the class on *why* that director does what he or she does and how that director can be one upon whose "shoulders you stand."
2. Make a list of what you are *passionate* about in the world of theatre. What do you want to do? What gets you up in the mornings with the excitement of "Hell, yes! I get to do *this* today!" Share and compare your lists in class.

3. Every director has (at least) one "Dream Show" in his or her head. Get a partner and take a few minutes to share your Dream Show. *Why* is it your Dream Show? Why do you want to direct it? What is your vision for that show? Does sharing the idea make it seem more or less daunting?
4. Consider the resources (physical, financial, and human) in the theatre department at your school. For the following shows, list whether or not it would be practical for your department to produce each one (make sure to explain why you answered the way you did).
   a. *Henry VI, Part I* by William Shakespeare
   b. *The Country Wife* by William Wycherley
   c. *A Doll's House* by Henrik Ibsen
   d. *The Cherry Orchard* by Anton Chekhov
   e. *Show Boat* by Oscar Hammerstein II and Jerome Kern
   f. *Oleanna* by David Mamet

Notes

1. Anne Bogart, *A Director Prepares—Seven Essays on Art and Theatre* (New York: Routledge, 2005), 14.

2. William Shakespeare, *The Tragedy of Hamlet, Prince of Denmark*, III, ii, 1–4.

3. Oscar G. Brockett, *The History of the Theatre*, seventh edn (Boston: Allyn and Bacon, 1995), 428–429.

Suggested Reading

Bogart, Anne. *A Director Prepares—Seven Essays on Art and Theatre* (New York: Routledge, 2005 (2001)).

Camus, Albert. *Caligula* (Paris: Gallimard, 1993 (1944)).

Chekhov, Anton. *The Cherry Orchard* (Cambridge: Cambridge University Press, 2006 (1904)).

Hammerstein II, Oscar (book and lyrics) and Kern, Jerome (music). *Show Boat* (New York: Rodgers and Hammerstein Library, 1927).

Ibsen, Henrik. *A Doll's House* (New York: Global Classics, 2014 (1879)).

Luce, Clare Booth. *The Women* (New York: Dramatists Play Service, Inc., 1995 (1937)).

Mamet, David. *Oleanna* (New York: Vintage, 1993).

Rostand, Edmond. *Cyrano de Bergerac* (1897, available online).

Shakespeare, William. *Hamlet* (*c.*1599–1602, available online).

Shakespeare, William. *Henry VI, Part I* (*c.*1591, available online).

Shakespeare, William. *King Lear* (*c.*1605–1606, available online).

Weiss, Peter. *The Persecution and Assassination of Jean-Paul Marat as Performed by the Inmates of the Asylum of Charenton Under the Direction of the Marquis de Sade* (usually known as *Marat/Sade*) (Chicago, IL: Dramatic Publishing Company, 1964).

Wycherley, William. *The Country Wife* (1675, available online).

11

CHAPTER 2

Skills
Directors Need

The skills a director needs are many and varied; ultimately, everything that you learn in your study of theatre (and your practice of theatre) becomes a tool in your toolbox. Creative skills, composition skills, organizational skills ... all of these are important and all should be honed each chance you get. However, there are three primary tools that every successful director must have and must continually work on to build and increase. None of the three is more important than the others; all require your constant attention. Because of that, I find it helps to think of them represented in the shape of a triangle.

For each of these skills, I could easily say, *this* is the most important one, but they are truly equal. Because of that, we could begin our discussion of them at any point on the triangle, but let's start at the top and work our way around clockwise:

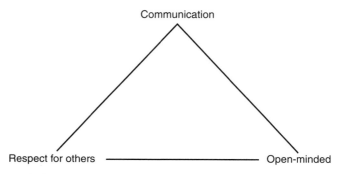

Figure 2.1 Skills of a director.

Communication

Remember our quote from *Hamlet* in Chapter 1? "Speak the speech, I pray you..." was Hamlet communicating his directorial desires to the Player King. In Anton Chekhov's *The Seagull*, Treplev tells Nina, "We should show life neither as it is nor as it ought to be, but as we see it in our dreams."[1] Showing your dream, telling your story, and displaying your directorial vision are all impossibilities if you cannot communicate them to your production team, cast, and crew. Whether in design meetings, rehearsals, or PR activities, everything you do as a director is going to demand excellent communication skills. And while there is no better way to work on communication skills than to practice communicating, there are three important keys you can think about to make sure you are communicating in the most effective way possible: phrasing, style, and knowledge/ excitement.

Phrasing

Picture this scenario: You are directing *Bus Stop* and you've had your initial design meetings with your production team to talk about your concept for the show. You go into your next meeting and your scenic designer begins to show her design. You look at it and say, "You need to put the kitchen up left and not down right." She looks back at you and says, "No." Now what? You are most likely angry at her flat refusal and considering what you need to say next to *make* her do what you want. You are at an impasse that seems divisive already ... and you've barely begun the process! Where did you go wrong, and how can you solve the problem? Better yet, how can you make sure that the problem doesn't crop up? It's all in the *phrasing*.

Look back at the previous paragraph and see what you notice about the director's phrasing; it should jump out at you once you look for it. Notice that, in the example, you've told the designer what she *needs* to do. By phrasing it that way, you've automatically set up a confrontational atmosphere that will be tough to overcome. When you are a director (or, really, in any leadership role), remember that questions are your friends. If, in our example, you phrase your initial desire as a question ("Could the kitchen be up left, instead of down right?") you have begun a discussion ... as opposed to an argument. Either the designer, when answering your question with a "No," will go on and elaborate her response, or if not you can follow up with the question, "Why not?" It is only then that you have the opportunity to learn that the water and electric hookups are behind the stage-right proscenium arch, and since you want your kitchen to be practical, it needs to be as close to the hookups as possible. Ahhhhh! A logical and good reason to roll with this altered vision to the design.

Designers aren't going to say "no" just for the sake of it. Remember that they work practically just as much as they work creatively and there will almost always be a logical reason for the answers they give you. If you are communicating in questions as opposed to declarative statements, it makes the collaborative process a much smoother one. I once directed a show and, after a technical rehearsal, was having drinks with one of the actors, who was also a director. He marveled at the fact that the set designer (with whom he had worked several times) and I were sitting next to one another throughout the rehearsal. He lamented that he could never get that designer to sit with him in rehearsals. I mentioned that I had often seen him going into the scenic studio of the theatre and *telling* the designer what he needed to do, whereas I would go in and chat with the designer each day—and not just about the show. We talked about current events, politics, sports, music, and other things, as well as the show. And because we had built a personal relationship with one another, that carried over to our professional relationship.

Style

"Communication" is a huge concept, with a range of aspects. It is important to know the style of communication you use most often, to make sure you are communicating in the most effective manner. Psychologist Claire Newton says, "Good communication skills require a high level of self-awareness. Once you understand your own communication style, it is much easier to identify any shortcomings or areas which can be improved on,"[2] so that you can communicate effectively in any situation. Newton and other analysts identify five primary communication styles: assertive, aggressive, passive-aggressive, submissive, and manipulative. While there aren't many submissive directors out there (at least, none who consistently get rehired), we have most likely all worked with directors who fall into the other four categories. Let's briefly examine the remaining four, in reverse order.

Manipulative directors are those who work indirectly to get what they want. They often secretly give notes to one actor, while ignoring the others, or pit members of the production team against one another, thinking that that will achieve the best results. The manipulative director will use guilt trips to get actors to come in and work outside of rehearsal, or pout when a costume designer won't change something when asked. Above all, manipulative directors rarely addresses an issue directly; instead they go around and around the matter at hand to accomplish what they want.

Passive-aggressive directors do a lot of complaining. They whine about not getting as much assistance from the front of house staff as all of the *other* directors get. They are sarcastic when giving notes to actors, often in (what they think is) a joking tone. Passive-aggressive directors will often feel put-upon, and make those feelings known, when producers or PR directors ask them to do something extra to promote the show. While passive-aggressive types might work well with a dictatorial artistic director or producer, they ultimately want everyone to know how difficult they have it and to feel sorry enough for them to give in to their way of doing things.

Aggressive directors are the "my way or the highway" types. They think that the best way to get actors, designers, and others to do what they want is to tell them what to do. And if that doesn't work, then they do it again—only *louder*. They may be great directors to have on board for meeting deadlines, but they can be difficult to deal with on a day-to-day basis. Rehearsals under an aggressive director typically involve a lot of shouting and a lot of arguments. Aggressive directors are usually hyper-competitive and believe that bullying and intimidation are the things that motivate those around them. Aggressive directors are loud, belligerent, and supremely confident that their way is not just the right way to do things, but the *only* way to do things.

Assertive directors are … direct. They are clear with their production team and actors on what they need and understand that having a conversation about those needs will result in the most positive outcome. They are also open to discussion and new ideas, realizing that there is always a different way to do things. Assertive directors lay out their plan and work to make sure that everyone is on board with it, while being flexible enough to recognize that plans often need to change, based on circumstances. Assertive directors make sure that everyone knows what is expected of him or her, and hold each person (including themselves) accountable.

After looking at the above list, it's pretty easy to tell which director you would like to work under, isn't it? Obviously, as presented above, assertive directors seem to be the best, and that is generally true. However, it's a fact of life that different situations call for different communication styles, and being able to utilize a little of some of the other three styles can be to your benefit. In a former life (long ago), I was a high school football and baseball coach. While the general opinion of coaches may be that they are all aggressive-style communicators, that isn't true of the best ones. The best coaches understand that you have to choose your communication style based on the situation and the people around you. Coaches have a saying about players: "You have to know whether to kick 'em in the butt or pat 'em on the butt." Though most coaches probably aren't thinking in terms of communication theory, they are recognizing the fact that everyone responds to different types of motivation, hence, communication.

Some actors want a director to tell them precisely what to do onstage: "Take four steps down left, look over your shoulder at him, and say the line then." Some want a director to leave them alone, essentially: "Enter up-right on this line" (with no other direction to follow that). Most actors fall between those two extremes. Some like to be given notes specifically and directly, while some get very self-conscious about notes and are afraid getting a note means they're "bad." Ultimately, you, as the director, need to understand what type of actors you have in your cast, and adjust your communication style, so that you can be most effective when talking with each of them.

Knowledge/Excitement

How can you communicate with anyone if you don't know your topic? That seems a rather basic and simple question, but you would be surprised how often it gets overlooked. The more you know about your show, the more research you've done (remember, research and reading…), the better prepared you will be to speak about your show. It doesn't matter if you're meeting with your production team, starting rehearsals, or speaking at the local Rotary Club luncheon, it is your responsibility to know your show inside and out.

Imagine you're directing a production of *The Hot l Baltimore*, and in rehearsals, the actress playing April asks you why her character seems to be so protective of Suzy. How are you going to answer that question? You need to know all the characters, all their relationships, all the situations they find themselves in. Only then will you be able to have the discussion with the actress in an effort to answer her question. If you don't have a deep, comprehensive knowledge of the play, any response you give will be shallow and won't do justice to what you are all trying to create.

Knowledge isn't enough; you have to be excited about your play. If you want people happy and excited to be working on this production, it starts from the example you set. When your cast and crew see and hear the passion you have for the show, that translates to them. Of course, you also want audiences to be excited about coming to see the show, and that excitement can be built through your promotion and marketing efforts when they see your feelings about it. When you are passionate about your project, it makes it so much easier to talk with others about it, because you want them to be passionate about it as well!

Communication is essential to your role as a director. If you are unable to communicate your vision, your goals, and your passion in an effective style, then the show will never have a chance at getting off the ground. But communication is a two-way street, and isn't just about you speaking. The other side of the coin is *listening*, and that's where our second point on the triangle comes in: being open-minded.

Open-Minded

If we accept that theatre is the most collaborative of all of the art forms, and that the director's job is the most collaborative one in theatre, that raises the question: How do I collaborate? It seems like an awfully basic question, but it's one that we don't often think about, unprompted. In an interview with Arthur Bartow, American director and co-founder of Arena Stage Zelda Fichandler said:

We have to teach ourselves and each other the art of collaboration, 'co-laboring' in order to express a collective consciousness—the fundament of the act of making theatre . . . It's necessary to do more . . . to think as ourselves and also as the others, to permit the perceptions and needs and priorities of the others to mingle with our own while preserving our separateness.

Zelda Fichandler[3]

When you approach a project in an open-minded fashion, what you are really doing is, as Fichandler says, allowing the "perceptions and needs and priorities of the others" join your own.

Too often, I see students begin a project, get a Great Idea, and then put that idea in a stranglehold and never let go. No matter how many times teachers, peers, or other collaborators make suggestions, they feel like their G.I. is *perfect*! Because of that, they see any critique as a personal attack and any suggestion for change as an attack against the Great Idea. This attachment to the Great Idea blinds them to other possibilities and serves as a barrier to collaboration, growth, and development. The G.I. can come in many forms: it might be a concept for a show, a casting choice, or perhaps it's a bit of staging. Regardless of the focus of the G.I., directors have to understand that what they do is all about looking at possibilities and making choices. Ultimately, it's not about making "right" or "wrong" choices, but distinguishing between choices that are "better" and "worse."

Let's say you are directing a production of *Disney's Beauty and the Beast*, and you've come up with a Great Idea for the ending fight between Gaston and the Beast, and the Beast's transformation into the Prince. You've decided that, in the final beat of the fight when Gaston stabs the Beast, their grappling can carry them over the edge of the castle wall platform, and the Prince can emerge from behind it after some nifty transformation lighting effects. Not only have you creatively solved the problem of how to accomplish the transformation, you've come up with a visually stunning ending to the fight. Brilliant! So, while you are staging this G.I. with your fight choreographer in rehearsal, the scenic designer (who has been watching rehearsal and taking notes) mentions to you that when she designed the castle set, she specifically visualized the final fight taking place on a different platform on the other side of the stage—one where the sculpting at the top is going to be different and, perhaps, allow for better sightlines for the fight. Now, the director who wants to protect the Great Idea at all costs will immediately dismiss the idea because it's not his blocking—his vision—his Great Idea. The smart director, though, the one who is open-minded and truly wants to "co-labor," will try it out. This director realizes that the designer may have a point, and it's worth spending some time in rehearsal looking at the fight in a different location to see if that choice might work better. Ultimately, whether you decide to change it or go back to the original staging, you've opened yourself up to the possibility of change. And by being open-minded to trying your scenic designer's suggestion, you've shown that you truly understand the spirit of collaboration. As an added benefit, you have also demonstrated the third quality on our triangle: respecting others.

Respect

As previously mentioned, any of the three points on the triangle could be considered the most important one, but this third point is certainly the most important when it comes simply to being a good human being—and really, that's what this is all about. Being a director means that you are a leader—whether you think of yourself as one or not—and good leaders must recognize the worth of others and show them respect. The best leaders are never "me first" kind of people. In Sophocles' play *Antigone*, Haemon tries (unsuccessfully) to make this point to Creon: "Do not believe that you alone can be right./The man who thinks that,/The man who maintains that only he has the power/To reason correctly, the gift to speak, to soul—/A man like that, when you know him, turns out empty."[4] You never want to be an "empty" director, thinking you are always right. Be a collaborator in every sense of the word, recognizing and respecting the talents and worth of everyone around you.

A trap that so many young directors (and many older ones as well) fall into is trying to do *everything*. Sometimes this is attributable to habit, as many directors start by gathering a bunch of friends together to put on a play ("Dad's got a barn—let's do a show!"). They get used to being director, stage manager, set designer, costume coordinator, and box office manager all at once. Because of that, when they begin working with an actual production team and a real budget, they still fall into old habits of trying to do every job—even though those jobs now belong to someone else! Sometimes, this is attributable to a fear that others won't be able to do things exactly the way the director envisions it. And sometimes, directors falling into this trap don't even realize that they're doing it; they're just so excited that they're running over everyone, almost unknowingly. Imagine you have been hired by the XYZ Theatre to direct *Fences*. So, you've been hired. Excellent! You know that, in hiring you, the producer has made a wonderfully insightful and intelligent decision by recognizing your many talents and offering you the job. And that is exactly the point: you have to trust that the same wonderfully insightful and intelligent producer who hired you exercised that same insight and intelligence in hiring everyone else! You must respect that they know how to do their jobs and trust them to perform exceptionally.

It's not just about showing respect for a person's job, but for the actual person. The production assistants, concession workers, ushers, box office assistants, carpenters, stitchers, and everyone else who works in the theatre all do it because they love it. They want to be a part of it. If you've made it this far in your academic life and are still pursuing theatre as a career choice, then you understand that it's not a choice people make for the money. People choose to go into theatre because they have passion for it—because the need and drive to be a part of an artistically creative process is so strong that they are willing to take on any role to be involved. Understand that about people: recognize that the same passion that fuels your soul is there in those around you. Remember, as Dr Seuss tells us, "A person's a person, no matter how small!"[5]

Exercises and Suggested Reading

Exercises

1. Read Claire Newton's full article on the five communication styles. You and a partner each make two lists: On one side, list your own behavioral characteristics (verbal and non-verbal) and conclude with what style of communication you most often use. On the other side, list the characteristics and draw the conclusion for your partner. Be honest. Share your lists with each other and discuss how you each see yourselves and each other. If there are discrepancies, discuss them.

2. You and a partner choose one of the scenes listed below. On your own, sketch a scenic design for it and then write out your blocking for the scene in the script. After you have finished, compare what you have done with your partner, and find a way to meld each of your visions together into one shared idea. Make sure to consider how you communicate your vision to your partner, and *listen* to your partner's vision. Discuss the process with the class.

    a. "The Balcony Scene," Act II, scene ii from *Romeo and Juliet* by William Shakespeare

    b. Brick and Big Daddy's "Mendacity" scene from Act II of *Cat on a Hot Tin Roof* by Tennessee Williams

    c. The final scene of *Miss Julie* by August Strindberg

    d. Part I, scene i of *Desire Under the Elms* by Eugene O'Neill

Notes

1. Anton Chekhov, *The Seagull*, I.
2. Claire Newton, "The Five Communication Styles," accessed June 15, 2015, www.clairenewton.co.za/my-articles/the-five-communication-styles.html.
3. Arthur Bartow, "Zelda Fichandler," in Arthur Bartow, *The Director's Voice, Twenty-One Interviews* (New York: Theatre Communications Group, Inc., 1988), 114.
4. Sophocles, *Antigone*, scene iii, 565–569.
5. Dr Seuss, *Horton Hears a Who* (New York: Random House, 1954).

Suggested Reading

Bartow, Arthur. *The Director's Voice: Twenty-One Interviews* (New York: Theatre Communications Group, Inc., 1988).

Chekhov, Anton. *The Seagull* (Chicago, IL: Courier Press, 2013 (1896)).

Inge, William. *Bus Stop* (New York: Random House, 1955).

O'Neill, Eugene. *Desire Under the Elms* (Reseda, CA: D'Arts Publishing, 2010 (1924)).

Shakespeare, William. *Romeo and Juliet* (1597, available online).

Sophocles. *Antigone* (*c.*441 BC, available online).

Strindberg, August. *Miss Julie* (1888, available online).

Williams, Tennessee. *Cat on a Hot Tin Roof* (New York: Dramatists Play Service, 1958 (1954)).

Wilson, August. *Fences* (New York: Plume, 1986).

Wilson, Lanford. *The Hot l Baltimore* (New York: Dramatists Play Service, 1998 (1973)).

Woolverton, Linda (book), Ashman, Howard and Rice, Tim (lyrics), and Menken, Alan (music). *Disney's Beauty and the Beast* (New York: Disney Theatrical Licensing, 1993).

21

CHAPTER 3

The Director's "Rules"

The brilliant theatre and opera director Peter Sellars has said about directing:

> I do material because I feel an obligation to the subject matter. Shakespeare wrote the play to get at certain subject matter. That subject matter remains on our minds, so let's talk. I try and create my productions as a discussion between ourselves and this play.[1]

In his quote, Sellars touches on several aspects that are important for directors to learn. Although, as mentioned before, there's no such thing as "A plus B plus C equals directing," there are certain "rules" that a director must learn and adhere to. These rules, rules, adapted from American director, Dr. Edmond Williams, are "macro" in a sense: think of them as guidelines, under which all of the rest of your job falls. No matter what project you're working on, as a director, you have three primary responsibilities: *make it work*; *everything matters*; and *tell the story*.

Make it Work

As a director, you will be faced with multiple problems each and every day. Some might be script problems, some might be actor problems, or design problems, or marketing problems, or space problems, etc., etc., etc. Whatever the problem is though, you have to Make. It. Work. That's it. That's the gig. Figure out the problem and address the problem. Now, obviously, you're not completely on your own and you do have tools at your disposal to assist you. To aid in discussion, we'll break the problems down into two categories: *script problems* and *production problems*. Although there is certainly some overlap between the two, and there are some problems that don't fit neatly under those umbrellas, this approach will help us look at them in a bit more detail.

Script Problems

The perfect play has yet to be written. Whether you consider *Hamlet*, or *Antigone*, or *The Cherry Orchard*, or *Death of a Salesman*, or *A Streetcar Named Desire*, or *Riders to the Sea*, or ... whatever as the greatest play ever written, none of them is perfect. If the perfect play were ever written, we could all just stop and go home; there wouldn't be any need to continue! So, accepting that premise, it stands to reason that every script you come across will have some problem points in it. Maybe it's something big, like a scene that doesn't work, or maybe it's something as small as a word that seems out of place. From the first time you pick up a script to read, you should be looking for problems that you know you will have to address. In the next chapter, we'll be talking about how to select and approach a script in a more specific fashion, so here we'll talk in broader sense. Read plays holistically and try to envision everything that you might possibly run up against as you move forward in production. And as you begin to identify problems, realize that you have certain things to help you address them.

23

Research (the director's best friend) will always be your most important tool. If you're not sure why a character says something, or if a certain line doesn't make any sense, those issues can turn into problems for you and your actors if you don't solve them. Most of the time, the research you do will help to answer your questions. One of the most famous of Shakespeare's soliloquies—Richard's opening lines in *Richard III*—is also one of his most confusing: "Now is the winter of our discontent/Made glorious summer by this son of York."[2] What is he talking about there? Is it winter? Is it summer? Who is this "son of ... York"? Is he talking about himself? Two lines into the play, you're already at risk of confusing your audience! So how, in fact, do you make this opening work without confusing everyone right from the start?

As a smart and insightful director (because, of course you are), you begin research into the meaning of these two lines. You know that your actor (who is also smart and insightful) will do his own homework, but as the director you need to be prepared to answer any questions that might emerge. Through your research you realize that seasonal metaphors crop up in Tudor poetry quite often, so for Shakespeare to start his play off with a seasonal metaphor fits into the convention of the time. You also discover that Shakespeare is very cleverly inverting lines that Thomas Kyd uses in the beginning of his play, *The Spanish Tragedy*: "But, in the harvest of my summer joys,/Death's winter nipp'd the blossoms of my bliss,"[3] with which the contemporaneous audience would certainly have been familiar. So very quickly you've discovered the poetic and artistic purpose of the opening, but what about the narrative purpose?

To discover the narrative purpose behind the lines, you start with a piece of punctuation—or, rather, the *absence* of a piece of punctuation: the end of the first line has no punctuation at all, creating enjambment that carries the thought over from line one to line two. In addition to the text on the page, you know (from your historical research), that Richard is referring to the end of the Wars of the Roses. This civil war, between the Houses of York and Lancaster, was covered in Shakespeare's three parts of *Henry VI*, and his audience would have known that. So, then, the "winter of our discontent" refers to the recently concluded civil strife, and the "glorious summer" is the victory by the "son of York," namely, Richard's brother the king—Edward IV. Additionally, the pun on son/sun works with the summer metaphor and the fact that Edward's symbol was a sun.

After just a little bit of research, look at the wealth of information you've uncovered! Some of it will be useful to the actor in helping him make sense of the lines; some will be useful to you as you navigate the script; and some will be useful to your audience, as you learn how to shape the production to help them understand the context of the show. We will be talking about research in more detail later, but know that research is one of your primary tools for addressing problems in the script.

Script analysis (Chapter 4) is another tool that will help you "make it work." The more detailed your analysis, the more comprehensive your knowledge of the play, and thus the better equipped you will be to address any challenges. Make sure you understand the dramatic function of each character and each scene. Why is a certain character present? What function does that character serve in the play? Why did the playwright include a particular scene? The answers to these, and many other questions, will provide the foundation for your approach.

Production Problems

The "Script Problems" category is pretty self-contained and also, pretty self-evident. Labeling the other category as "Production Problems" really is a catch-all for "everything else." These could be problems in marketing, or staging, or costuming, or ... anything. Any number of things can fit under this umbrella. Of course, in an ideal world, you will have a marketing director, a technical director, a costume designer, and more, whose primary responsibility will be to address the problems in these areas, but remember that the proverbial buck stops with you. It's your ultimate responsibility to make sure that *everything* works. I always tell students that you don't have to *be* a scenic/costume/lighting/props/sound/etc. designer to direct, but you have to know enough about each area to be able to hold intelligent discussions with each designer. Also, in most smaller companies, the director is a key ingredient in marketing the show so your input will often be encouraged. Finally, the path that most directors take in their careers involves at least a few "guerrilla theatre" productions where you serve as a "one-person band." So being able to recognize and address problems in all of these areas is going to be vital.

Script analysis is a big tool in addressing production problems as well as script problems. Character breakdowns, scene breakdowns, technical breakdowns, and shift plots are all tools that will allow you to deal with logistical problems that may crop up in your show. As mentioned before, you should read plays holistically, looking for any and all problems that might crop up. Your breakdowns will help you find those moments that may be difficult for actors, or the crew, or for you! Remember, everyone needs to know who is onstage and whether they should take or leave the sardines when they hang up the phone![4]

The old real-estate cliché of "location, location, location" is vitally important to you as well. Many production problems will affect your staging, and knowing the layout and design of your space is paramount. Not just what the scenic design will be, although that is obviously vital, but the actual architecture of the theatre. Where will the performers be in relation to the audience? What type of stage will you be using? Proscenium? Thrust? Arena? Flexible? As you read your script, you should be thinking about the traffic patterns your blocking is going to create and where actors will need to be. What problems might arise? How will you make it work? If you're

25

directing *Greater Tuna*, then you have two actors who, between them, are going to have over 40 costume changes. The type of stage you'll be working on will dictate much of the flow of your show, as you need to make it work for each of the actors (and their dressers!). Assume that you've blocked the show to be performed on a thrust stage, but after a Kennedy Center American College Theatre Festival response, you find out your production of *Greater Tuna* has been selected to go to the regional festival (hooray!!). Your initial excitement dims a bit when you discover that all shows performed at the regional festival take place in a large proscenium house. How will you adjust your staging and design to accommodate that change? Your creativity and vision will have to be flexible enough that the show performed at festival is just as good as the performance in your home theatre.

The examples and possibilities of problems that might arise truly are limitless. The key for any director to know, though, is that the final responsibility lies with you. Find the problem. Fix the problem. Obviously, you will never be able to identify every potential problem that a show might provide, but the more you can anticipate, and the more flexible you can be in addressing the problems, the more effective you will be. It's important to understand, too, that some problems will simply be out of your control. You will have to recognize what you can and cannot fix, and be sure to address everything within your power in an effort to make it work.

Everything Matters

My wife is an arts administrator, a stage manager, and a perfectionist, which makes her critiques of my work as a director invaluable, since I know her comments are coming from a professional perspective and not an "oh, honey, that was cute" perspective. She never talks about whether she likes a show or not; she always talks about what she noticed during a performance—because that's her job. Of all of the shows I have directed over the years, her favorite was a production of *Dearly Departed* by David Bottrell and Jessie Jones. After the show, she had only two comments: first, an actress used a compact that was the wrong style for the 1970s; and second, there was a price tag left on a potato chip bag. She did not mention any of the performances, or the direction, or design ... only the compact and the potato chip bag. The point, of course, is that *everything* matters when you are directing.

Figure 3.1 A scene from *Dearly Departed*, featuring the offending potato chip bag, *sans* price tag. (L–R: Amy Updegraff Heinz, Leigh Anne Chambers, Andrea Newby, Rebecca Riisness, Susan Leming Eastus. Photo courtesy of Mark D. Guinn, and the Louisiana Tech University Department of Theatre.)

There is an idea in communications theory that says a message does not have any meaning until it is assigned one by the person receiving it. While the concept is a little esoteric, its application to you as a director is not. No matter what you intend when you direct a show—no matter what message you want the audience to take away—you never know what they are going to notice. Nothing is too small for your attention, and you can bet that someone somewhere will see the tiniest detail. Unfortunately, you never know what will be the focus of any given audience member. Some simply watch the actors and focus on the story. Some audience members like to look at the actors who are not at the center of attention. Some will look at the lights, or costumes, or set, or props, etc. As the director, you have to pay attention to all aspects of the production, not just the acting.

In *A Director Prepares*, Anne Bogart recounts a story of a graduate directing student who replies to an actor's question about the placement of the chair with "It doesn't matter." She goes on to say: "Something matters to an audience only if you make it matter. If you attend to it, if only for a moment, the commitment of your attention will create the tension of attention."[5] The reality is that you will always miss something: no one is able to catch every single mistake or problem. However, your goal should be to notice as many as humanly possible. You want to make sure that everything that goes on the stage has been given your attention at some point, so that there are no "mistakes" up there for the audience to find. Each part of your production should be a conscious choice on your part.

There are times that your choice is to leave a "mistake" in. It could be budget or time constraints that limit you, or perhaps the space itself forces you into choices you would rather not make. Regardless of the reason, if you are aware of the problem areas and are able to say, "Yes, I know that should be different, but we're going to go with it," then you're making it a choice. Obviously we want audiences to like our work, but sometimes we have sections of shows that we know someone might not like, appreciate, or understand. As long as that's been a conscious choice on your part, with the realization that it might not work for the entire audience, but you can live with that, then you're doing your job. Just make sure that you are making the best choice possible.

I once directed a production of *Jesus Christ Superstar* at an outdoor theatre. The space is absolutely gorgeous, nestled in a natural amphitheatre at the top of a hill. The gigantic stage is constructed against a sloping hill of pine trees that make for a beautiful setting. Dominating stage right is one of the largest scenic elements you've seen: a 30-foot-high rock structure that has been built to include several paths and "cave" entrances, all the way to a top plateau that is roughly 25 feet in diameter. Now, intelligent theatre student that you are, if you were to be directing that show, where would you stage the crucifixion scene? On top of the gigantic rock, right? Naturally, that is where the scene took place in our show ... until the producer came to the first dress rehearsal. When we got to that scene, she leaned over to me and said, "No. Oh no. You can't do that up there." When I asked her why we wouldn't want to use the most dominant scenic element on the planet for the climactic scene of the show, she said she didn't think the company's insurance policy would allow it. She did, however, agree to have the insurance person come and watch the final dress rehearsal the following day. As you have, by now, I'm sure, surmised, the insurance person confirmed that we could not stage that scene up there. The insurance rider stipulated that nothing or no one could be lifted above the top level of the rock platform, and of course the cross for the crucifixion lifted the actor playing Jesus a few feet above the top level. Even when I pointed out that the actor would have to untie his own arms from the cross, jump down, and either roll or run 15 feet to get to the edge of the platform, our insurer was not moved (or particularly amused by my imagery, I might add). So we restaged the scene, putting the cross down on ground level, and leaving the audience to wonder why we weren't using the gigantic rock for the crucifixion. It was certainly something the audience noticed (obviously an extreme example) and asked about. It was also certainly not the ideal staging, but it was something I was able to defend as having been a conscious choice, and the best one available to us.

Tell the Story

Every play has a story. Some plays tell grand and complicated stories of murdered fathers, revenge quests, and usurped thrones (*Hamlet*), and some tell simple and humorous stories of newly divorced bachelors learning how to live with each other's idiosyncrasies (*The Odd Couple*). Your job as the director is to find the story and tell it. Every decision you make must be based on telling the story. You must ask yourself with each choice you make: "Is this the best way of telling the story? Is this the most effective way to tell the story? Is there another way to tell the story? Am I telling the story in the manner in which I desire?" Many people have a difficult time differentiating story from plot, but remember that *story* and *plot* are not the same. You can think of the plot of a play as a skeleton, and the story of the play as everything else that makes up a person: muscles, tendons, ligaments, blood, skin, hair, etc. etc. The plot is the framework on which everything else is built. As a director, you will certainly need to concern yourself with plot (that is what much of your script analysis will entail), but your *job* is to tell the story of the play. Many directors, regardless of age or experience, make choices about their productions for gratuitous, lazy, or disconnected reasons. Whether you're talking about a great big choice—like whether to change the setting for Shakespeare's *As You Like It*—or a small choice—like how to get a prop onstage—you have to make sure that the choice you are making serves the story.

29

With its pastoral themes setting up a contrast between city and country life, *As You Like It* is one of Shakespeare's more malleable plays in terms of setting. There are many eras and locations that could serve for a production that seeks to transfer the show away from Shakespeare's original setting, but it can't justifiably be placed in *any* setting. Putting the show in a hippie commune in 1973 works well, as much of that late-twentieth-century movement eschewed urban societies. In the first scene of the play, Charles, discussing the location of the usurped Duke, says:

They say he is already in the Forest of Arden, and a many merry men with him; and there they live like the old Robin Hood of England. They say many young gentlemen flock to him every day, and fleet the time carelessly, as they did in the golden world.[6]

Those lines give one of the first clues in the play that the story can be told in the context of "free love" and "live and let live," as epitomized by hippie culture. Setting the play in a German concentration camp during World War II, however, will definitely *not* produce the same results. The setting doesn't work for the story, which means that anyone choosing to place the play there is doing so either out of ignorance or to accommodate an agenda that doesn't truly go with the play (as an aside, I have seen both of those locations used as settings for *As You Like It*).

The first possibility mentioned above—ignorance—can be remedied by a director who does sufficient research and study before deciding on a concept for the show. The second, however, is more problematic. Directors who make poor conceptual choices, such as the example above, often have their agenda or concept decided upon prior to selecting a script (or being hired to direct). If you've predetermined a concept or approach, then you are not serving the story at all; rather, you are attempting to make the story serve you. By doing that, before you've even begun the real work of directing, you are in danger of missing the boat entirely. Choices you make shouldn't be gratuitous (unless they serve the play); they shouldn't be made simply because they are funny (unless they serve the play); they shouldn't be made to serve your agenda (unless they serve the play). You get the point. If you are directing a production of *The Odd Couple*, it is not wise to direct your actors to play an undercurrent of sexual attraction and frustration between Oscar and Felix, in an effort to make a postmodern statement about sexuality and divorce … that has nothing to do with the story! Even the most studious of English majors would have a tortuous time coming up with logic to justify that choice, and if you're having to reach that hard for a justification you have most likely erred.

Just as stories can be big or small, depending on the play, your choices (and whether or not they work) can be big or small.

Regardless of the import of the choice, though, you have to make sure that it is helping you tell the story in the best way possible. All my students know a phrase that I use to illustrate this: "Don't drop a baby from the grid." I once worked on a production of *The Marriage of Bette and Boo*. A running gag in Christopher Durang's macabre comedy about an extremely dysfunctional family sees the cast lining up next to the wings several times, as a doctor brings out and delivers a dead baby for them to see. The final leg of the gag (and the final dead baby) is traditionally just tossed onstage from the wings. Throughout rehearsals, I pestered the director to drop the final baby from the grid, and not just toss it onstage from the wings. I argued that, if it was funny sailing on from the wings, then how much funnier would it be plummeting from 15 feet over everyone's heads. After days of refusal, and to shut this eager young artist up, the director agreed to try my idea during a technical rehearsal. The moment came: eagerly anticipating what I was sure was going to be a simply hilarious moment, I leaned forward in my seat in the house. The sandbag-and-doll's head "dead baby" dropped from the grid, hurtled toward the stage, and arrived with a satisfying (and sickening) *thud*. The entire production staff, all the actors, and all the technicians exploded into laughter. I looked at the director, however, and said, "I get it." The baby never dropped from the grid again. While it was morbidly funny—even hilariously so—it destroyed the mood of the scene by taking the joke one step too far (and farther than the playwright intended). The actors were unable to regain their focus or control after that moment, and if the actors couldn't do it then we never would have regained the audience had we left that in the show. The lesson the director was seeking to teach me was that just because something is funny doesn't mean it should be put into a show—even if the show *is* a comedy.

31

The lesson Mary Shelley taught us in *Frankenstein*—that just because we can do something doesn't mean we should do something—applies to directors as well as scientists. This goes for all of the decisions a director must make during the course of a show, and not just those in the above examples. Directors should bear this rule in mind when working with designers as well. With new technological advances made almost daily, there are a wealth of gadgets available to designers. As you work with designers in meetings and during productions, keep asking yourself (and the designer) if the choices you are both making are telling the story in the best way possible. Just because you have a new intelligent lighting instrument that can be assigned to a particular actor and programmed to follow that actor at all times, it doesn't mean you have to use it. You could find that the use of such technology distracts the audience from the action onstage and they wind up focusing on the light, as opposed to what the actor is doing and saying. While the light may be gorgeous, it ultimately has to work in service to the story being told by the play. And that is true of *all* parts of the production—from casting, to design, to conceptualization, to moment-by-moment interactions, to the program design—they all have to serve the play and *tell the story*.

Exercises and Suggested Reading

Exercises

(For each of the exercises below, assume you are directing a production of *Richard III*.)

1. Fill in the "character—scene—location worksheet" for each act and scene (duplicate the page as needed, to create a sheet for each act). As there are over 40 characters listed in the script (before getting to "attendants, ghosts, servants, etc."), you will need to double and triple-cast several roles. Use what you discover by filling out the worksheet to list which roles you can have single actors play.
2. Decide on a setting for your production. Make a list of up to ten songs that you will use as pre-show music. Next to each song, write a brief note justifying that choice (remember, everything you choose matters). Discuss your list with the class.
3. Choose a setting or concept for your production (different from the choice you made in Exercise 2). Using examples from the play and any preliminary research you need to do, justify your choice. Discuss your approach with the class.

Notes

1. Michael Billington, "Peter Sellars," in Maria M. Delgado and Paul Heritage (eds), *In Contact With the Gods? Directors Talk Theatre* (Manchester, UK: Manchester University Press, 1996), 231–232.
2. William Shakespeare, *King Richard III*, I, i, 1–2.
3. Thomas Kyd, *The Spanish Tragedy*, I, i, 12–13.
4. Michael Frayn, *Noises Off* (New York: Samuel French, 2004).

5. Anne Bogart, *A Director Prepares—Seven Essays on Art and Theatre* (New York: Routledge, 2005), 59.

6. William Shakespeare, *As You Like It*, I, i, 100–103.

Suggested Reading

Bottrell, David and Jones, Jessie. *Dearly Departed* (New York: Dramatists Play Society, 1998).

Delgado, Maria and Heritage, Paul (eds). *In Contact With the Gods? Directors Talk Theatre* (Manchester, UK: Manchester University Press, 1996).

Durang, Christopher. *The Marriage of Bette and Boo* (New York: Dramatists Play Society, 1985).

Frayn, Michael. *Noises Off* (New York: Samuel French, 2010 (1982)).

Howard, Ed, Williams, Jaston, and Sears, Joe. *Greater Tuna* (New York: Samuel French, 1983).

Kyd, Thomas. *The Spanish Tragedy* (*c.*1582–1592, available online).

Miller, Arthur. *Death of a Salesman* (New York: Penguin Books 1976 (1949)).

Shakespeare, William. *As You Like It* (*c.*1599, available online).

Shakespeare, William. *Richard III* (*c.*1592, available online).

Simon, Neil. *The Odd Couple* (New York: Samuel French, 2010 (1966)).

Synge, John Millington. *Riders to the Sea* (*c.*1898–1903, available online).

Webber, Andrew Lloyd (music) and Rice, Tim (lyrics). *Jesus Christ Superstar* (New York: Rodgers and Hammerstein Library, 1970).

Williams, Tennessee. *A Streetcar Named Desire* (New York: Signet Classics, 1986 (1947)).

33

PART II

PREPARATION

CHAPTER 4

Approaching a Script

The previous chapters have examined general ideas and responsibilities for directing; the rest of the book now moves on to address directing more specifically. What is it that directors *do*, and how do they do it? Obviously, it all starts with the script, but wonderful scripts that you burn to direct don't simply fall out of the sky (wouldn't it be lovely if they did?). Research and analysis of scripts is at the heart of your job as a director, before you ever hold auditions or begin rehearsals. However, before you even make it to those steps, you have to find the right script. "Right" is a relative term, depending on your personal taste, your location, the company you are with, and countless other variables. This chapter will examine how you, as a director, deal with a script, focusing on each step in the process.

Script Selection

Whereas research and script analysis go hand in hand, and you will wind up doing both of those things at once, script selection is an individual process. It would be wonderful if we could simply choose any script that strikes our fancy to direct, but of course things don't work that way. Many times in your career, you will be a kind of "mercenary" director, i.e. you are hired to direct a show that has already been selected (and perhaps already cast), but there will be times when you have the primary voice in the selection process. For those times, there are five things you need to consider when looking for a script:

1. Personal attraction;
2. Target audience;
3. Location;
4. Produce-ability;
5. Budget.

1. *Personal attraction.* Obviously, we're not talking attraction in the physical or romantic sense. By "personal attraction," I mean you need to find a show that you have a connection to on some level. It can be a show that you love and have always wanted to do, or a script by a playwright you admire, or a play that tells a story about which you are passionate, or any number of things. The important thing is that you feel a driving *need* to direct this play. It should be something that speaks to you and has a story that you want to tell. If you are, however, working a gig as a "mercenary" director, then this may be one of the most difficult areas. Oftentimes directors take a job because we need the job—simple as that. Whether or not we *like* the play has nothing to do with it. In those cases, you have to find some "hook" that can get you into the play, because without some kind of attraction to the piece you

Figure 4.1 A portion of the opening of *Disney's Beauty and the Beast.* (Photo courtesy of Riley Coker and the Oklahoma Shakespearean Festival.)

will never give the show your best effort. Years ago, I was hired to direct a production of *Disney's Beauty and the Beast*, and at the time, I had absolutely *no* interest in the show. However, I needed the gig and it was with a company that I really wanted to work for, so I took the job. Knowing that I had to find that hook, I dove into the script. I immediately noticed that the opening of the show was a beast of its own kind! With dozens of characters parading through town and being introduced to the audience, all while singing a deceptively difficult song, it was a huge staging challenge and one that intrigued me. That challenge became my hook, and before I was done the show wound up being one of my favorite jobs!

2. *Target audience.* For whom is the play going to be produced? It seems a simple question, but it's one that, surprisingly, many directors do not consider. Whether they think this is a question for a producer or a marketing director, or whether they just don't concern themselves with the audience, too many directors make a mistake by ignoring it. Script selection must take the audience into consideration. Knowing the target audience of your theatre—whether a professional company, educational theatre, community or church theatre, or freelance group—is paramount. What is the mission statement of your company and does the script fit with it? Are you selecting a show that goes into a themed season? Is your company dedicated to producing new works? Classical plays? Musicals? Is it a show for children or will it be marketed to families? What are your audience's expectations, based on previous productions by the company? Is there a specific push by your company to build new audience members? The answers to all of these questions will help you answer the larger question of your target. If your theatre company's mission is to cater to kids and families, then you might want to put down *Caligula* and pick up a copy of *Annie* when you're choosing your script.

3. *Location.* As previously mentioned, the real-estate axiom of "location, location, location" applies to script selection and directing. This consideration is tied in closely with the question of target audience, in that it requires you to have an understanding of where you are producing a show. If you are directing at a theatre or college in a particularly conservative

39

region, you should give strong consideration to any potentially controversial aspects of your choice of script. This is not to say that you as an artist shouldn't push the envelope, but in the real world you need to have a good idea of *how far* you can push it. If you are directing at a church-owned college, for instance, it would be foolish to ignore that when selecting a season. The important thing for any director to do is to make sure that you are having a conversation with administrators, executive directors, board members, or anyone else along the food chain who has final approval. You will find that they will appreciate your conscientiousness and you will save yourself potential headaches. You also may discover that the envelope can be pushed farther than you thought. While teaching at a private, church-owned college, I was considering programming Arthur Miller's *The Ride Down Mt. Morgan*. Late in the play, Theo, who is a deeply religious woman, has a bit of a breakdown and says: "I can say 'fuck' you know. I never cared for the word, but I'm sure she has her limitations too. I can say 'fuck me, Lyman; fuck you' whatever."[1] Concerned about whether or not it would be acceptable to produce for our department, I consulted the Dean of the College (who was an ordained minister). He simply asked me if it was an important part of the show, to which I replied in the affirmative. He then encouraged me to move forward with the production. Though surprised to get the approval, I never would have known had I not asked. The lines of communication must be kept open, and a director has to understand everything about the situation.

4. *Produce-ability.* Excuse the portmanteau, but there's no other easy way to refer to whether or not your company can successfully produce a script. Considerations for this topic include your talent pool, your space limitations, your technical abilities, and your staffing. If you have a small pool of actors who can't carry a tune in a proverbial bucket, you might want to think twice before selecting *Into the Woods*. If your performance space is a ten-by-ten, dead-hung black box, then *Les Misérables* is most likely not your best choice. If your design and tech staff consists only of a single lighting designer, then you might not want to pick *Joe Turner's Come and Gone*. Selecting the right show for you and your audience and your company is great, but if you don't have the ability (talent, technical, or

otherwise) to produce the show, then you've set yourself up for failure. Make sure that you are considering all of these aspects of production when you are selecting scripts to produce.

5. *Budget.* You might think that this should be the first consideration, but as an artist, you often have to rely on your creativity to "make ends meet." Most young directors begin their careers with the guerrilla (or "Dad's got a barn—let's do a show!") approach. You find a group of friends who want to produce something, and then go about finding a bar, storefront, park, or parking lot where you can do it. In these instances, you truly are making the most with the least, and finding creative solutions to work with no budget at all. Once you progress in your career, don't forget the creative spirit that you started out with. If there is a show you have found that meets the first four criteria, then trust that your collaborators are creative enough artists to find a way to make it work. Of course, if we could completely ignore budget, then it wouldn't be on this list at all. Since it is, however, there are some budgetary considerations you must make. If you're working for an education, community, or church theatre, then the budget question is almost strictly limited to production costs. How much money can your company afford to spend on rights, royalties, design, build, etc.? Every organized theatre will have a budget for a production, and although as a director you may not be directly responsible for administering that budget, you do need to be aware of it. If you are working for a professional company, then in addition to the above costs, you have to take into account salaries and benefits. Again, as a director you may not be directly responsible for administering those costs, but you must know what they are. If you're working for a small summer theatre that has the budget for a ten-person company, then selecting *The Government Inspector*, with its 20+-person cast, isn't particularly wise.

When you do have the opportunity to choose your own script (or at least take part in the selection process) make sure to consider each of these five elements as you read scripts. You will read a *lot* of scripts— there's not a successful director out there who doesn't. The more you read and stockpile scripts, the more ideas you'll have when a producer comes to you and asks, "What show would you like to direct?"

Remember, as we've said again and again, reading and research are the director's best friends. Speaking of research, that brings us to the second element of approaching a script.

Research

"Research is formalized curiosity. It is poking and prying with a purpose. It is a seeking that he who wishes may know the cosmic secrets of the world and they that dwell wherein."[2] So wrote the famed American author, Zora Neale Hurston, in her autobiography. You've read throughout the book so far about the importance of research, and here we'll look at what to research and how to go about it. In Chapter 3 you learned that "Everything Matters," and that carries over to your research. As a director, you really do have to research everything possible. You may wind up discarding much of your research, but you won't know what will be useful and what you can discount until after you actually *do* the research. Directors all have their own ways of researching a production, with some taking much longer than others. Some directors will spend a year or longer researching a show, while others will only take a week or two. Some directors like to immerse themselves in their research, covering their offices in pictures that relate to the show, running videos on a loop, and only listening to show-appropriate music. Some directors like to spend hours and hours in the library for their research, while others do (most of) theirs online (the Internet age makes researching a show *much* easier than it used to be, but make sure you are using trusted websites). Whatever style of research you use and however you go about it, have fun and engage your curiosity; discover the cosmic secrets of the play, as Ms Hurston suggests.

Though there are as many ways to go about researching a production as there are directors, what follows is a great foundational approach to the process. An easy way to illustrate the areas you need to research is to think in terms of concentric circles. This concept is called the "director's matrix." The idea of the matrix is that there are various levels of information that you should research (see Figure 4.2).

The inner ring is the world of the playwright. This is the world in which the playwright lived (or lives, for those still with us), and includes everything from the politics of the time, to social mores, to cultural and artistic creations, to architectural and clothing styles (and more). This is important because you need to know and understand the backdrop to the playwright's work. Every day we are

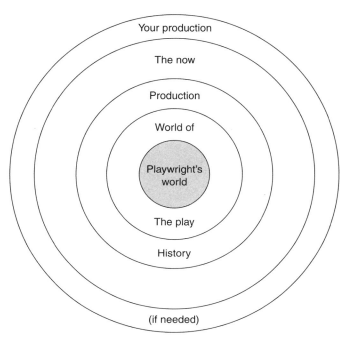

Your production

The now

Production

World of

Playwright's
world

The play

History

(if needed)

Figure 4.2 The director's matrix.

influenced by the world around us in tiny ways about which we are often consciously unaware; the same is true for playwrights. Art does indeed hold a mirror up to nature, and that mirror reflects the world in which every playwright lives. As such, you have to make sure that you fully understand the things that influenced the playwright in writing your script; that understanding will allow you to make better-informed choices as you begin your work.

The second of our circles is the world of the play itself. In some cases, when playwrights write about contemporary events, this might be the same—or at least similar to—the world of the playwright. But even when a play's subject is contemporary to its writer, there are still differences to explore. If, for example, you were directing Douglas Carter Beane's comedy, *The Little Dog Laughed*, your research into the world of the playwright would focus on early-twenty-first-century New York City, where Beane lived when he wrote it. Your research into the world of the play, however, would focus on early-twenty-first-century Hollywood, where the play takes place. Yes, there are similarities, but there are huge differences between New

York and LA. Of course, many plays take place in settings that differ wildly from the world of the playwright. Whatever the case is, though, your work is to research and understand the world that the playwright has created for the story.

Moving outward, we next come to the world of the production's history. Assuming you are not working on a new script, or one that has not been produced (and if you are, you can skip this part), you need to look at what other directors have done. You're obviously not looking to replicate their work, which would be highly unethical. (Directors have no way, as of yet, to copyright their work: it is almost impossible to guard yourself and your productions against creative plagiarism. This is something that will hopefully be addressed one day. Those future lawyers among you who are using an undergraduate degree as a primer for law school: get on that, would you?) Your research here is to see how other people have handled the show and how earlier productions were received. Previous reviews, interviews with creatives, features, and more can be great resources for you in this section of research. The production history research can help you understand what makes a show successful (or not) and why it might be worthy of a remounting ... particularly *your* remounting. Typically, you will want to limit your production history research to professional productions (London, New York, regional theatre around the US), but occasionally you may find there has been a production closer to home that you might find useful. Again, you never know what research you don't need until you actually *do* the research.

The next ring in our matrix is the world of the now. Because theatre is a living art form, all performances take place in "the now." While your research at this level may not be as deep as the previous two, you do need to make sure that you study and are aware of how your own contemporary audiences will react to a play based on the world in which they live. This can become extremely important when doing a period piece whose meanings may be interpreted completely differently by today's audience than by its original audience. In Noël Coward's *Private Lives*, there is an absurd amount of smoking and drinking, which, while appropriate to the style, is received differently in today's context (especially since many theatres don't allow smoking onstage at all). Additionally, the play revolves around a theme of almost casual domestic violence—all played for laughs—that very likely resonates quite differently for today's audiences. Toward the end of the second act (and before they get into a physical fight onstage), Elyot and Amanda lovingly recount a previous bout:

> AMANDA. That was the first time you ever
>   hit me.
> ELYOT. I didn't hit you very hard.
> AMANDA. The manager came in and found us
>   rolling on the floor, biting and
>   scratching like panthers. Oh dear, oh
>   dear. *(She laughs helplessly)*[3]

Though of course the scene fits perfectly for the style and time period, and plays humorously within the context of the show, domestic violence is a subject about which society is now much more aware than in the first half of the twentieth century. Any director assaying the script will have to understand the context of the now and how this show might play for today's audiences.

The final circle of the matrix won't necessarily be used for every show you direct. This ring—the world of your production—is only applicable if you layer a concept onto the show. To go back to our earlier example of setting *As You Like It* in a hippie commune in 1973, the outer circle would be vitally necessary in that production. Your initial research would include the world of Shakespearean London, the French Court and Forest of Arden, and your own world. For your production, though, the added matrix level of 1973 hippie communes becomes important as well. If you are directing the show without altering its setting and without adding an elaborate concept, then this outer ring of the matrix will not be necessary.

For each level of your research you have a multitude of options available as source material, both online and in hard copy. Articles, reviews, books from the time period, music, architectural journals, clothing catalogs, photographs, and interviews are all excellent resources. One of the keys to successful research is making sure you have a variety of sources; otherwise the information you gather is likely to be one-dimensional and won't serve you particularly well. As you research, it's helpful to keep individual file folders with the information you gather. Some directors like to print out and keep hard copies of everything, though I find that electronic filing works best. At most theatres where I direct, we use a shareable service (Google Drive, Dropbox, or an internal server) so that all members of the production team have access to research that might be helpful to them. Whether sharing with others or simply keeping a copy of

45

your research on your hard drive, make sure that you label each section and file folder so that you can find what you want easily. You don't want to be four weeks into rehearsal, have an actor ask a question, and think: "Hmmmmm, I know I read something about that. Now where did I save it?" Regardless of how you research, remember that it will be an ongoing process throughout your show. Don't neglect your research simply because you have begun rehearsals: you never know when you might find *just* the right nugget of information to open a new door of understanding for you or your actors.

Script Analysis

Earlier in the chapter, I noted that script analysis tends to go hand in hand with research. The reason is that both these aspects of directing have a somewhat symbiotic relationship. As you analyze your script, you will find questions that will need to be researched. As you research, you will find ideas that will assist you in your analysis. There's probably a tortured metaphor about analysis being the peanut butter to research's chocolate in the Reese's Cup that is preparing a script for production, but I won't make it in case I'm just hungry right now. Oh, you're hungry right now too? I'm glad it's not just me. In any case ... script analysis.

There is no single "correct" way to go about analyzing a script. As with so many aspects of our art, everyone tends to develop their own methods and approaches. The ultimate goal, regardless of the approach you take to script analysis, is to ensure that you have as much knowledge of and information about your play as possible. Remember, once you start rehearsals, you will have the shiny little faces of happy and curious actors turning to you to as if to say, "What in the hell does *this* mean?" Your analysis will allow you to answer those questions, or at the very least to reply with "I'm not sure, but I have some ideas. Let me go back and look at my analysis and I'll let you know." Remember (and this is only a tad off-topic), it's never a bad thing to answer a question with "I don't know," as long as you follow that up with "... but I will find out and let you know the answer."

The method of analysis you will find here is an excellent foundation for those learning to direct, or a differing viewpoint for those who have been directing and want to try something new. As you work through it, you will find areas that make perfect sense to you and some areas that are completely obscure and present difficulties.

Regardless, explore each of these categories fully, and you'll have an excellent knowledge base from which to work on your show. Script analysis is divided into five categories, with each of those categories further separated into individual topics. We will look at each of them in depth, but first, the categories we break analysis down into are:

1. Structure;
2. Story;
3. Character;
4. Text;
5. Overall.

Many directors like to read a play once, just for pleasure, before beginning the analysis process. Reading it through and letting your brain wander around while doing so can be a great way to stimulate your creativity. After that, your analysis starts in earnest. Begin your script analysis with the "five reads" exercise. Before getting into serious detail analyzing your script, read it through five times. With each reading, hold one question from one of the categories in the forefront of your mind about the play (this will make a bit more sense once you see the descriptions of each of the categories). For example, if I was preparing to direct *Ruined*, by Lynn Nottage, I might read it first with the question of how the play is organized (a *structure* question) in my mind. The second read might have me focusing on whose story is being told in the play (a *story* question). Next, I might read it looking only for the relationships between central characters (a *character* question). The fourth read would see me focusing solely on characteristics of the dialogue (a *text* question). Finally, I would read it while asking myself what I think is the central image of the play (an *overall* question). By starting off with the five reads, you are becoming familiar with the text in a detailed fashion, and preparing yourself for the detailed analysis that follows, as you examine each of the following categories and topics:

1. *Structure.* Structure deals with the shape and format of a play. How has the playwright set the play up and what can I, as a director, learn from that? This first step in the analysis, while seemingly basic, provides vital information that you will use as you approach design meetings, auditions and casting, rehearsal scheduling, and promotional activities. Each of our categories is divided into five topics for further analysis. In the

category of structure, here are the detailed topics you should explore:

a. *Organization.* How has the playwright organized the play? Is it broken into acts and scenes? Is it left as one big chunk of text? Earlier in the book, you used the "character—scene—location" worksheet, which presupposes that the script is broken into acts and scenes in a traditional manner. However, not all plays are; if not, then you will need to find some way of dividing it up. Either create your own act and scene breaks based on dramatic action, or use "French scenes" (the process of denoting scene breaks using the entrance or exit of principal characters). You need to chart the organization of the play to understand how it all fits together. The organization is going to be your roadmap for understanding the way that the play works and will help you as you begin setting up your rehearsals.

b. *Settings/locations.* How many settings are used in the script? Where are the locations? When looking at that question, don't merely look at interiors vs exteriors, but look specifically at the locations in the script. Your designers will certainly be doing the same thing, so this will put you on an even footing when you are in design meetings. Also, knowing where and how many locations there are will enable you to assist your actors in the early stages of rehearsals as they are building their characters and seeking to understand their relationship to their environment.

c. *Characters.* Speaking of characters, that is your next topic of exploration. How many characters does the playwright include? What are their ages? How many are male and how many female? Are there transgender characters? What about gender-neutral characters? Are there characters who could be cast as any gender? Obviously, the discoveries you make on this topic will tell you a lot about the play and its story, but, in a more immediately practical sense, these discoveries will help you as you prepare to conduct auditions. You need to have a strong sense of how many (and what type) of actors you need as you enter auditions.

d. *Stage directions.* How does the playwright use stage directions? Does the script include long, detailed, and descriptive stage directions like those of Tennessee Williams? Or does it use brief, utilitarian directions like the scripts of David Mamet? What do the stage directions tell you about the play? Do they provide the given circumstances and the exposition? Do they describe the characters? Are they present to help set the mood or describe technical effects? Do they provide blocking or acting cues? The first thing many directors do (and instruct their actors to do as well) is take a black marker and block out all of the stage directions in the script. The thought process behind this is that if they follow the stage directions they are somehow ceding their creative authority. Remember, though, the playwright has put the stage directions in because that is the way he or she saw the play unfolding writing it. As a director, you don't have to feel tied to the stage directions, but you don't automatically have to throw them out either. Find what is beneficial to you within the stage directions. Sometimes, stage directions are there because others who have worked on the script before you figured out the best way for something to happen. In those cases, there's no need for you to try to reinvent the wheel by automatically dismissing them.

   e. *Special features/needs.* This category can encompass a wide variety of needs. Is the play a musical? Is there dancing? Does it call for stage combat or firearms? Do the characters have to eat onstage? What about cook? Does the play call for live animals to be a part of the show? Or puppets? With this category, you are looking for anything that is out of the ordinary with the script. What elements does the show involve that will, in some way, need to be factored in to your work? Perhaps these features will affect design choices, or casting, or rehearsal structure, or something else entirely, but they are elements that you are going to have to deal with as you begin to work on the show in earnest.

2. *Story.* In Chapter 3, you learned the importance of telling the story as a director. But before you can tell the story, you have to know what the story is! Not only do you need to understand the story, you need to make sure that the story you want to tell is the same as the story that is in the script (you'd be surprised how often some directors fight against the story of

the play in an effort to tell their own, unrelated story). To explore the category of story, you will need to look at the following topics:

a. *Given circumstances.* The given circumstances are the "facts" of the play, as provided by the playwright. Those facts may be communicated through author's notes, stage directions, or dialogue. Every play will have its own set of given circumstances, but it's important to remember that each scene within a play can have its own given circumstances as well. The given circumstances that you need to look for and address include:

   i. Environment. Where are we? When are we? What are the political, social, economic, and religious influences?

   ii. Previous action. What has happened before the start of the play (or scene) that impacts the play itself? Remember that theatre is a contrived art form and we must deal with it differently than we deal with "real life." Instead of a straight and linear path, with plays we often have to work backwards.

   iii. Exposition. The exposition is the information that the playwright provides that we *have* to know in order for the play to make sense. Some playwrights put their exposition in a neat, tidy bundle at the beginning of the play (Henrik Ibsen). Some spread their exposition out over long stretches—or even the entirety—of the play (Eugene O'Neill and Tennessee Williams). Many playwrights combine those two approaches. Finally, some playwrights, such as Harold Pinter, provide little to no exposition, and force you to confront the action of the play on its own merits.

b. *Whose story is it?* Too often, directors miss this point. A play is made up of characters, which means that the story being told has to belong to (at least) one of the characters. Sometimes, the answer to this question is fairly obvious. *Hamlet* is about the young Prince of Denmark. Amazingly, it is usually with these types of plays that directors put on their black turtlenecks, berets, and sunglasses and say in a condescending tone, "Ahhhhh … but really this play is about Ophelia and her struggles as she is pulled between her father, her brother, and her lover." *No!* When you see those directors, you should slap them—metaphorically speaking, as I am not one to advocate physical violence. The play is *not* called *Ophelia*. It's called *Hamlet*. Don't be obtuse. Obviously, not every play provides an answer to this question so clearly. You may find characters who share the story, or that the answer to whose story it is changes throughout the play. Whatever the case, you need to make sure that you know whose story you will be telling with your production.

c. *Dramatic action.* In his wonderful book on script analysis, *Backwards and Forwards*, David Ball notes that a "play is a series of *actions*. A play is not *about* action, nor does it *describe* action ... a fire *is* flames. A play *is* action."[4] Earlier, I mentioned that we often have to work backwards when exploring a play; examining dramatic action is the perfect example of this. In the "real world," the chaos that is our minds spits forth desires and thoughts. Those desires and thoughts coalesce into words and actions. In a play, we're given the words and the actions, and have to work backwards to find the thoughts and desires that precipitated them. The dramatic action is tied to the structure of the play. By looking at the way the playwright organizes the script (which you've already done in the first category), you begin to see the shape of the dramatic action. When analyzing the dramatic action in detail, use the following steps:

    i.   Identify the inciting incident. This is the catalyst for the action of the play, the moment that sets the ball rolling (Hamlet sees his father's ghost, who sets him on a path of revenge. Lear decides to divide up his kingdom based on his perception of his daughters' love for him).

    ii. Divide your script into units. Think of a unit as an expansion of an actor's "beats." A unit would be a completed thought or action within the script. When a new topic or character is introduced, or when a thought or moment is completed, you have a new unit. Mark your units in your script, and give each one a title. The title should be a brief representation of the action found in that unit. An example would be "the Confrontation" as a unit title for Hamlet meeting his father's ghost.

51

iii. Identify the primary action of each character in a scene. To do this, you simply ask the simple question: What is the character doing in the scene? The answer you are seeking is a literal one, don't try and make it too difficult. In "Practical Aesthetics," the acting style developed by David Mamet and William H. Macy, there is a concept called the "popcorn test," and this is a good way to think of it. If you and a friend are at a movie and you step out to get some popcorn, you might come back to ask your friend, "What's going on?" Because you are in a movie theater, your friend answers in the most direct way possible: "He's trying to convince her to fly to Paris with him." It's a simple declaration of the primary action for the scene. Remember that the primary action of one character may be in opposition to the primary action of another ... which is where you find your conflict. If you *don't* find the conflict in the characters...

iv. Find the conflict. Remember that, without a conflict, there's no story. Identify the source of conflict for the story, whether it is man vs man, man vs beast, man vs nature, or man vs himself. Or perhaps, it is some combination of these.

v. Look for the cause and effects. Many directors like to express action in terms of "A does something to B, which results in C." Ball refers to these as "triggers" and "heaps," with the idea that an action precipitates a responding action. Whatever terminology you want to use, what you are really doing is establishing the causal relationship of events in the script. This is called a "cause-effect chain." An example of a cause-effect chain, using *Hamlet*, would be:

> *Claudius kills Old Hamlet → Hamlet comes home for funeral → Hamlet stays for wedding → Hamlet sees ghost → Hamlet begins to act "mad" → Claudius suspects Hamlet → Hamlet shuns Ophelia → Polonius gets involved → Claudius brings in R & G → Hamlet hires the players → Hamlet doesn't kill Claudius while*

"praying" → *Hamlet kills Polonius* → *Claudius sends Hamlet away* → *Ophelia kills self* → *Hamlet switches letters to cause deaths of R & G* → *Hamlet and Laertes return* → *Hamlet and Laertes fight at grave* → *Laertes and Claudius conspire against Hamlet with poison* → *Hamlet and Laertes duel* → *Everybody dies* → *Fortinbras takes over Denmark.*

These chains can be used for the play overall, using broad events of action, and then can be successively narrowed down and used for individual acts, scenes, French scenes, and units.

d. *Rhythm/pace.* Every play has its own rhythm. As we talked about in the *structure* category with length, the rhythm helps dictate how the show will flow for your actors and for your audience. As you identify the rhythm of the show, you will learn how to help your actors pace their performances. Just as a character has a *primary action* for each scene, the story being told has a *primary moment* in each scene. This is the most important event in the scene (and yes, some scenes may have more than one but rarely will a scene contain more than two). By identifying the primary moment for each scene, you can determine pacing and rhythm.

If you look at Figure 4.3, you see a simple graph, indicating acts and scenes along the *x* axis and the number of pages in each scene along the *y* axis. By marking the page in the scene where the *primary moment* occurs, you can begin to see a shape. In the example, the first-act scenes all have their primary moments in roughly the same area. This indicates an essentially steady rhythm to the act. In the second act, the primary moment for each

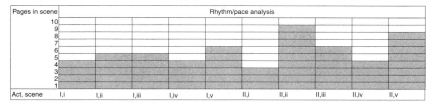

Figure 4.3 An example of a rhythm/pace chart.

scene jumps around pretty drastically, showing that the pacing will be much more erratic. For those who don't want to make the chart, you can simply highlight the primary moment for each scene in your script. The important thing is that you, as the director, understand where each of them falls, so you can shape the rhythm of your show.

  e. *Arc.* By the time you have completed your analysis of the first five elements of *story*, you will be able to see the arc of your show. How much time is spent on exposition? How long does it take the action to build? Where does the climactic moment (or moments) fall? Does the action and conflict have a resolution at all? How long does it take to get to it? Knowing the arc will ensure that you understand how the show has to flow, in order to tell the story in the most effective way possible.

 3. *Character.* As Ball noted, a play is action. The action, of course, is performed by (and to, and at, and with, and other prepositions) the characters. Actors are taught, when developing their characters, to learn as much about them as possible, and develop them in as much detail as possible. While directors won't go into *quite* as much detail about each character as an actor would, you still have to study the characters in your script, and, unlike an actor, you have to do it over and over, for each one. So how do you go about your character analysis as a director? You will need to look at the following six topics:

  a. *Status.* In every scene, the characters will have a status that is relative to the other characters. Typically, we simply break it down into "high," "middle," or "low," though you can further delineate the categories if you choose. It is important to note, though, that this category is not looking at social status. In many scenes, you'll find the Nurse has a higher status than Juliet, regardless of the fact that she is a servant in the Capulet household. This type of status deals with who is "driving the scene." Which character is aggressive and which is passive? Which character is in charge? Which character is seemingly biding her time? Identify the status for each character in each scene.

  b. *Function.* One of the things I always stress to young actors is the importance of understanding the dramatic function of your character. *Why* is your character in the play? What purpose does the character serve? For directors, it's no different. You must understand the purpose that each character serves in the play. Some will be the owners of the story. Some will be the observers of or reactors to the story. Some characters serve as a surrogate for the audience and some characters are present merely for expository reasons. Figure out and note the function of each character in your script, and remember that a character's function can change from scene to scene.

c.   *Relationships.* Understanding how each character relates to every other character in the play is vital, and will ultimately assist you in every other facet of your directing. Your analysis can certainly turn, based on the relationships of characters, but the actual work you do in rehearsals will as well. By understanding the relationships, the way you block and shape scenes will be supported and allow you to make the best choices in the visual telling of your story. The simplest way to discover the relationships between the characters is to do a character web.

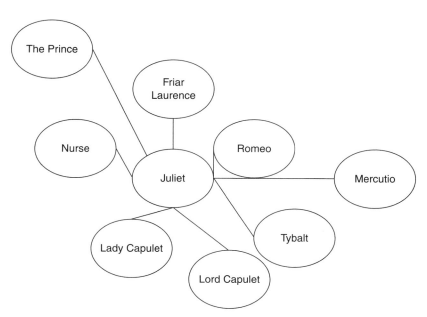

Figure 4.4 Sample character web for Juliet.

As you can see by the example (Figure 4.4), the character web is a quick way to illustrate the relationship each character has to others. For Juliet, you see that her closest relationship is to Romeo, with the Nurse and her mother closely following. Moving outward from the center, Friar Laurence and her father occupy the next level, with Tybalt and Mercutio connected to her relationship to Romeo. The Prince, obviously, is far out for Juliet, but he does have an impact on her. After completing the character webs for your principal characters, you will have a *much* stronger grasp of how everyone fits together.

d. *Objectives and obstacles.* The heart of all actor homework also has to be part of your analysis as a director. What is each character's *super objective*? What is their objective hierarchy? What (or who) are their obstacles? You will need to answer these questions for each character, to assist your actors and answer potential questions they might have. The strategies and tactics can be left to the actors, but you will need to discover the answer to these questions for yourself.

e. *Arc.* Another acting point that directors should know is the arc of each character. Much like you analyzed the arc of the story, a character's arc helps you to understand the shape and pacing of each character. Where are the important moments they must face and deal with? How do they change (positively or negatively) from the beginning of the show to the end? Make sure to know each character's journey.

4. *Text.* The text is where we find the most information in any script: more than the stage directions or character descriptions, it is the text that is the key to everything that happens in the play. In addition to being the vehicle for telling the story, the text tells us about each of the characters, carries the action of the play, and is the essence of the artform. It may seem odd that the text gets its own category, since every other aspect of script analysis is rooted in the *textual* analysis, but there are fantastic elements you can glean by focusing on the text alone. When speaking in broad terms, and for the purposes of the analysis, I tend to use "text" and "dialogue" interchangeably, though there are obvious differences between the two. The topics, then, for your textual analysis are:

a. *Structure of dialogue.* In many ways, particularly if you are working on a classical piece, analyzing the structure of the dialogue is simply looking at the way it is laid out on the page. In Shakespeare (and other classical drama), a quick glance tells you if you are dealing with verse or prose. Look at these two examples from *Henry V*:

> CHORUS: Oh, for a muse of fire that
> would ascend
> The brightest heaven of
> invention!
> A kingdom for a stage, princes
> to act,
> And monarchs to behold the
> swelling scene!
> (I, i, 1-4)
> WILLIAMS: You pay him then. That's a
> perilous shot out of an
> elder-gun, that a poor and
> private displeasure can
> do against a monarch! you may as
> well go about to
> turn the sun to ice with fanning
> in his face with a
> peacock's feather. You'll never
> trust his word
> after! come, 'tis a foolish
> saying.
> (IV, i, 250-255)[5]

Examining structure is helpful for other styles of dramatic literature as well. Does the playwright use long, flowing, and descriptive phrases like Tennessee Williams? Short, choppy, and interrupted phrases like David Mamet? Direct and pointed phrasing like Paula Vogel? Is the text primarily dialogue? Monologues? Soliloquies? Sung? Additionally, who is doing the talking? Which characters carry the line load in a given scene? All of this structural analysis of the text will show you the ideas and characters that the playwright finds most important.

b. *Function of dialogue.* In the same way we talked about understanding the dramatic function of a character, you should explore the function of dialogue as well. What is the purpose of each character's lines? To indicate function of dialogue, use the infinitive form of a verb to describe each line. This is a common method that most actors will be familiar with, as it's an excellent way to clarify and condense each line's purpose. The simplest way to notate this is by writing in the margins of your script, though some directors prefer to keep a separate sheet with the line verbs on it. As an example, go back and look at the dialogue belonging to the soldier Michael Williams from Act IV of *Henry V* that was used in the previous section. Though there are a variety of options you could choose, perhaps the best verb to delineate function would be "to insult." Remember that you are crafting these based on your understanding of and desires for the text. Your actors may come up with others, which then provides an excellent point of discussion and opportunity for character growth.

c.   *Word choice/syntax.* How does the playwright decide to have the characters speak? What do the choices of the words they use tell us about the characters? What about the sentence structure and syntax—what can we discern about the characters from those choices? For many playwrights, the word choice, syntax, grammatical structure, etc. that a character uses is about poetry, musicality, and artistry. But we can also gain insight into a character by the way he or she talks. Why does Juliet say that a "rose by any other name is still as sweet," instead of saying "Why could you not be from some other family?" While the alternative phrase conveys the same meaning in a clearer and more direct fashion, it not only loses the poetry of the original line's metaphor but fails to reflect the character Shakespeare wrote in Juliet. The original line is a line that would be spoken by a lovesick, impetuous, early-teenage girl and does a much better job of reflecting her mental and emotional state in the scene. All of that, from one simple phrase!

d.   *Characteristics of dialogue.* What does the dialogue *sound* like? How does/should it roll off the tongue and hit the audience's ear? What are the various rhythms the characters use when they speak? Do any of the characters have particular words or colloquialisms that they use? Repeated phrases or words? Does any of the text represent or call for dialect? These questions are meant to get you thinking about what the audience is going to hear and how they might respond to it.

e. *Imagery.* How are images used by the playwright and how are they expressed through the text? Are there recurring images? Are there shared images (between characters)? Are they direct or obscure? Are they literal representations or figurative? Seek to utilize the images you find as the link between the text itself and your vision of the play.

5. *Overall.* After you have completed the first four categories of your script analysis, you will have an excellent handle on the play and all its parts. This final category allows you to synthesize your discoveries and pull your vision back out to a more macro level. The analysis up to this point has been for you to dig into the "nuts and bolts" of the script and primarily serves you in your understanding of the play. Those categories will contribute to your discussions with others, but that is not their main focus. The overall category will allow you to think in broad terms and will provide a foundation for discussion with collaborators, as well as those outside of the production process. You can think of this category as providing you your "talking points" for interviews or promotional work.

a. *Idea.* Simply put, what is the play about? (My answer to this is always "About two hours." Har har.) This question works on the literal level, as it refers to the plot and story—how do the events of the play express the idea(s) of the playwright? But it also works on a more figurative level—what are the implications of events in the play (the subtext) and how do those express the idea(s) of the playwright? In addition to examining the ideas found in the action, characters, text, and subtext, examine the title of the play closely. Sometimes, the idea of a play is expressed as part of the title. Shakespeare's *Twelfth Night or What You Will* has a wealth of information in the title alone. The traditional twelfth night feast of Epiphany was marked with an inversion of the social order, and this spirit of "anything goes" permeates the play.

b. *Philosophy.* What philosophical statements are brought to light in the play? Sometimes your research into the world of the playwright or the world of the play will reveal the play's philosophy. Some playwrights, like George Bernard Shaw, come straight out and state their philosophy in a foreword or afterword, or have a character who does it for them, like Alfred Doolittle in *Pygmalion*:

> What am I, Governors both? I ask you, what am I? I'm one of the undeserving poor, that's what I am ... my needs is as great as the most deserving widow's that ever got money out of six different charities in one week for the death of the same husband.[6]

Most other playwrights aren't nearly as direct as Shaw, but look to discover the characters, lines, and moments in the play that illustrate the philosophy behind it.

c. *Atmosphere.* Many directors consider "atmosphere" and "mood" to be interchangeable. Regardless of which word you prefer, there is a trap that many directors fall into: namely, they try to pick the atmosphere they feel the play *should* have, instead of looking for the atmosphere that the play *does* have. Atmosphere (or mood) arises from the script. You cannot pre-select an atmosphere, or you will risk imposing something on the script that isn't there. Playwrights, directors, and designers all manipulate atmosphere, but you have to see what atmosphere is suggested by the play first. Make sure you are thinking beyond the literal and appealing to all five senses with your atmospheres. Go through all of your units, and next to each unit title, choose an adjective that best describes the atmosphere for that unit.

d. *Central image.* So much of the analysis that we do as directors involves concrete excavation of the script. Determining the central image of a play allows you to engage your sense of creativity and metaphor. After completing all the previous sections of the analysis, synthesize what you have learned and come up with a single image that, for you, represents the entire play. Similar to Chekhov's "psychological gesture," the central image is the *essence* of the play for you. If you were directing *Macbeth*, you might decide that your central image is a grasping fist. Or, for

Romeo and Juliet, two caged songbirds (should they be dead songbirds? Is that too much? Actually, if that's the image the show conjures for you, then no, it's not). Your central image should be strong, and representative of the play as a whole.

e. *Audience.* Back at the beginning of this chapter, we talked about the importance of knowing your target audience when selecting a script. As we conclude the chapter and our section on script analysis, we come back to the audience. This time, though, you are looking for the audience the playwright was writing for. Who was the *playwright's* target audience? For contemporary plays, this usually isn't a difficult question, though it can be. Lin-Manuel Miranda's musical, *Hamilton* (which premiered on Broadway in 2015) begins with the character of Vice-President Aaron Burr rapping: "How does a bastard/Orphan/Son of a whore and/A Scotsman/Dropped in/The middle of a forgotten/Spot in/The Caribbean by Providence/Impoverished/In squalor/Grow up to be a hero and a scholar?"[7] Is he writing for rap fans? Historians? Kids? Adults? It's your job to figure out which (spoiler alert: in that case, the answer is probably "all of them"). Older plays, however, can be a little more tricky. You have to look at the audience that would have been contemporary to the playwright and ascertain what would have been common knowledge and may not be to *your* audience. If you are directing *The Rover* by Aphra Behn, you must look at all the aspects of the play that Behn's audience would have known—references, implications, situations, etc.—and determine how (or if) you will make those accessible to your audience. Remember, the audience is the reason you're telling your story in the first place!

Most directors I know tend to have a love/hate relationship with the process of preparing a script to go into production. They love the scholarship (because most directors are scholars in some way), but they begrudge the fact that they haven't yet gotten to the "fun part" of directing—which is the rehearsal period. Though it may be long, and occasionally tedious, the work you do in preparation for auditions and rehearsals will be the foundation for your entire production. Once you finish with it, you will find it to be invaluable.

Exercises and Suggested Reading

Exercises

1. Choose a season for your school's theatre department. Make sure you take all five steps into consideration. Bring in your selections for the next class period and be prepared to discuss and justify your choices.

    (For the following exercises involving research and analysis, it is recommended that the instructor select an easily accessible ten-minute play script for the class to use. O. Henry's "While the Auto Waits" or August Strindberg's "The Stronger" are good options. Another possibility would be to select a single scene from a full-length script.)

2. Using the play selected for your class, research the *director's matrix* and complete the directing research worksheet found on the website. Compare what you found useful with others in your class. Make note of sources and items you might have missed.

3. Perform the "five reads" exercise described in the chapter for the play selected for your class. Remember that with each reading, you are focusing on a *single question* to answer with that reading. Jot down notes of your discoveries and share with the class.

4. Use the play selected for your class to complete the script analysis worksheet, also found on the website. Remember that some portions of the analysis will need to be noted in the script. Compare results with others in the class. Take note of differences of interpretation and analysis.

Notes

1. Arthur Miller, *The Ride Down Mt. Morgan* (New York: Dramatists Play Service, 1999), 61.

2. Zora Neale Hurston, *Dust Tracks on a Road* (Philadelphia, PA: J. N. Lippincott, 1942), 143.

3. Noël Coward, *Private Lives* (New York: Samuel French, Inc., 1975), 34.

4. David Ball, *Backwards and Forwards* (Carbondale, IL: Southern Illinois University Press, 1983), 9.

5. William Shakespeare, *Henry V*, I, i, 1–4 and IV, i, 250–255.

6. George Bernard Shaw, *Pygmalion*, II, 256–257, 260–261.

7. Lin-Manuel Miranda, *Hamilton*, "Alexander Hamilton."

Suggested Reading

Ball, David. *Backwards and Forwards* (Carbondale, IL: Southern Illinois University Press, 1983).

Beane, Douglas Carter. *The Little Dog Laughed* (New York: Dramatists Play Service, 2007).

Behn, Aphra. *The Rover* (*c.*1677, available online).

Boublil, Alain and Schonberg, Claude-Michel. *Les Misérables* (New York: Musical Theatre International, 2009 (1980)).

Coward, Noël. *Private Lives* (New York: Samuel French, 1975 (1930)).

Gogol, Nikolai. *The Government Inspector* (1836, available online).

Hurston, Zora Neale. *Dust Tracks on a Road* (Topeka, KS: Tandem Library, 1996 (1942)).

Lapine, James (book), Sondheim, Stephen (music and lyrics). *Into the Woods* (New York: Musical Theatre International, 2009 (1986)).

Meehan, Thomas (book), Strouse, Charles (music), and Charnin, Martin (lyrics). *Annie* (New York: Musical Theatre International, 2004 (1976)).

Miller, Arthur. *The Ride Down Mt. Morgan* (New York: Dramatists Play Service, 1999 (1991)).

Miranda, Lin-Manuel. *Hamilton.* Available as Miranda, Lin-Manuel and McCarter, Jeremy, *Hamilton: The Revolution* (New York: Grand Central Publishing, 2016).

Nottage, Lynn. *Ruined* (New York: Theatre Communications Group, 2009).

Shakespeare, William. *Henry V* (*c.*1599, available online).

Shakespeare, William. *Twelfth Night, or What You Will* (*c.*1601–1602, available online).

Shaw, George Bernard. *Pygmalion* (1912, available online).

Wilson, August. *Joe Turner's Come and Gone* (New York: Plume, 1988 (1984)).

63

CHAPTER 5

Auditions and Casting

You've selected the script. You've researched the script. You've analyzed the script. So now it's time to begin the production process with auditions and casting your show. Depending on the show and the company for which you are working, directors don't always have the opportunity to cast their shows. Larger companies (and some smaller) will often employ a casting director, or the artistic director or producer may handle casting. However, many times you will have the opportunity to run the auditions and cast your show. In those instances, it takes a great deal of thought and consideration on your part to complete the kind of "human Jenga" that casting a show requires. If you do have the opportunity to set up and run the auditions, you have a variety of options regarding the type of audition. Let's start, then, by explaining and then looking at some of the pros and cons of different types of auditions.

The Monologue Audition

What is it? The monologue audition is one that expects the actors to have a monologue (or two) prepared to perform. This style of audition is common throughout educational and community theatre and is also used in "cattle-call" and unified auditions that have multiple companies auditioning a large number of actors, but is no longer typically used in New York and other large markets that are holding show-specific auditions.

What are the pros? The biggest benefit of the monologue audition is that you are seeing the actors at their best. They are performing a piece (or pieces) that they have worked on, polished, and are extremely comfortable with, and therefore can showcase themselves for the auditors.

What are the cons? The biggest drawback to this audition type is that you are not getting to see the actors in direct relation to your play. While you can request that they perform a monologue from the play you are directing, it may be that there aren't enough monologues in the script for actors to use. So often, with this type, you find yourself casting Nicky Silver's *Fat Men in Skirts*, but watching an actor perform a monologue from Beth Henley's *The Miss Firecracker Contest*. The disconnect can sometimes be difficult to overcome.

The Cold Read

What is it? The cold read audition has the actors coming in without a prepared piece. They are given sides from the script when they arrive at the audition, and a short amount of time to look over the scene before being asked to read for the auditors. Sometimes the actors will read with a scene partner, and sometimes they will act with a "reader," a member of the production staff who reads with each actor individually.

What are the pros? The cold read audition allows you to see the creative genesis of the actors. This type of audition forces actors to make immediate choices about character and situation. You have the opportunity to see which actors are open and able to make big, bold choices, and also which actors are able to take direction and make changes on the fly.

What are the cons? Some actors, as you know, simply don't do well on initial reads. Perhaps you've been in shows before where you've sat in the first read-through and thought "Jeez! How is that person going to play this role?" Of course, a week later, you could never imagine anyone else playing that part. Some actors work best after they've had time to digest and assimilate a role. Because of this, there is a possibility with this type of audition that you miss out on actors who could be great in a role.

The Prepared Audition

What is it? The prepared audition is almost a combination of the previous two types, and is the type that you will find most often in New York and larger markets. In this style of audition, sides are made available ahead of time for actors to read and study before coming to the audition. They are then prepared to read a scene from the show that you have chosen. Again, depending on the set-up, the actors may be reading with a scene partner or a reader.

What are the pros? In this style of audition, you are seeing the actors read directly from the show you will be casting, and they are doing so having had the chance to study and think about the character and the situation (at least, to some extent).

What are the cons? Typically, in these auditions, the actors are only coming in reading for one role. Because of that, you may have difficulty envisioning them in any of the other roles for which they might be suited.

The Specialized Audition

What is it? Well, to begin with, it's a name that I just made up! I use the term to serve as an umbrella for any show for which you will need to see actors do specialized performances: sing, dance, fight, etc. In a musical, you will typically have the actors do one of the three initial types of auditions mentioned, and then they will sing (the standard is 16 bars from a song). Assuming there is dance involved, you will often have a choreographer or assistant choreographer to teach a combination for the actors to perform. For shows that involve stage combat, you may want to have a portion of the audition dedicated to seeing how well they can move, or pick up simple fight choreography.

What are the pros? The most obvious benefit is that you are getting an early glimpse into what skills the actors auditioning have, in addition to acting. Do you need a juggler for your production of *Robin Hood*? Then it's good to see who can *actually* juggle, as opposed to those who just have it on their résumé.

What are the cons? There really aren't any artistic drawbacks to this type of audition. You need the opportunity to see the actors perform these skills, and this is the way to do it. The only real negative is that specialized auditions are, by their very nature, longer in duration.

The Callback

What is it? The callback audition is a second audition where you have narrowed down the list of actors you want to see again. In terms of format, callback auditions can be whatever you need them to be. Some directors like to see a different monologue, some will have sides for the actors to read, and some will provide sides for the actors who are called back to study ahead of time. For musicals, many directors use the callbacks to hear the actors sing or see them dance more.

What are the pros? The callback gives a director an opportunity really to work with the actors and get to know them a bit better. Because you are dealing with a smaller group of people, you are able to take more time with each actor. Also, you can pair actors up, to begin to get a feel for their chemistry with one another.

What are the cons? Some directors spend too much time in the callbacks and wind up asking too much from the actors. They get so involved with the scene, and are so excited about the production, that they wind up treating the callback like a detailed character rehearsal. The result of this is having actors who come out of the process exhausted, confused, or just plain bitter.

Regardless of the type of audition you choose to hold, remember that, as a director, you *want* the actors to do well. Nobody wants to sit through three hours of wretched auditions. With that in mind, make sure that you are doing everything you can to make the audition process a warm and welcoming experience for the actors. Smile at them as they take the stage. Take a moment to speak to them. Call them by name, and thank them for their work when they've finished. You'll be amazed at how much goodwill can be engendered by basic courtesy and kindness. That goodwill carries over to future auditions and you become known as a director whom actors want to audition for, one they look forward to working with when they see your name attached to a production.

Whichever type of audition you settle on, you will eventually have to cast your show. Casting is, in many ways, an art form in itself. I wish there were a magic bullet I could offer to make all your casting decisions brilliant, but unfortunately that doesn't exist. Some plays are very specific in their casting needs (the lead in *Rocky, the Musical* should probably look like a boxer), and sometimes a playwright will

67

describe what a character should look like in the script. With plays that include a character who needs a specific look, it's fine to use that as a guideline, but you should be wary of character descriptions. Remember that playwrights writing character descriptions are describing an ideal that works for them, but may not necessarily work for your production. So, in many ways, you are on your own once you approach auditions. There are, however, a few things you can do that will aid you in the casting process. As you move into auditions, you can break your casting considerations into three areas: Prior to auditions, during auditions, and post-auditions.

Prior to Auditions

The first decision that you need to make as you prepare for auditions is how you are going to cast your show. What is going to be the driving force behind your casting decisions? Are you casting to fit your concept? Are you casting based on look? Compatibility? Are there certain qualities—like specific ethnicity, singing, dancing, or stage combat experience—that are required of any characters, which will dictate your casting choices? We always tell actors to not try to second-guess casting decisions, because they can never really know what is going into the director's decision-making process. It usually isn't until an actor takes a directing class and gets to sit on our side of the table that they truly understand that, though. While it may be natural to think that the most talented actor gets the role, that isn't always the case. As you can see by some of the questions above, you may have other priorities in making your decisions. Your answer to those questions is going to limit your talent pool before you even get to the auditions, so let's examine them.

Are you casting to fit your concept? If you have layered a concept on top of your show, you may find it necessary that your casting choices fit within the range of that concept. A (somewhat extreme) example would be if you decided to do an "inverted" production of Shakespeare's *Othello*, where Othello would be played by a white actor, with all of the other characters played by actors of color, as performed at the Shakespeare Theatre in Washington, DC in 1997, with Sir Patrick Stewart playing the Moor. Obviously, your casting choices for the show would be different than if you were doing the show "traditionally." Other concepts that would dictate your casting choices might be a musical in which you decide that the actors will be their own orchestra, as in John Doyle's 2005 production of

Sweeney Todd, or utilizing hearing-impaired actors in the manner of Deaf West's Broadway productions of *Big River* in 2003 and *Spring Awakening* in 2015. Regardless of what your concept is, remember when deciding on it that it will profoundly affect your auditions and casting.

Are you casting based on look? There will be some shows that either demand a certain look for certain characters, or you will decide that you want a certain look for certain characters. The aforementioned *Rocky* should have a boxer type as the lead. Or, you may decide that, in your production of *Midsummer Night's Dream*, you want Oberon, Titania, Puck, and the fairies to look like supermodels in an effort to set them apart from the human characters in the play. Still other shows might see you choose to cast actors who look good (or "right") together in roles that share time on stage—whether that's a family resemblance for Amanda, Tom, and Laura in a production of *The Glass Menagerie* or having an Albert and a Rosie who look like they should be a couple in *Bye, Bye, Birdie*. In any of these cases, you will find yourself passing over talented actors who just don't have the necessary look for your production.

Of course, the issue of colorblind and non-traditional casting comes in here as well. Colorblind casting has become the norm in most theatres around the country, and because of this the talent pool has greatly broadened from what it was 10, 20, or 30 years ago. Be open-minded when you are casting, and even if look is one of your primary factors, expand your thinking to include as many actors as you possibly can. A word of advice, though, when it comes to color-blind casting. Some roles really do require a certain race or ethnicity for the show to work. In the aforementioned production of *Othello*, if every actor in the show looks the same, and Othello doesn't stand out as "the other" in some sense, then the show misses much of the point. If you don't cast white actors in the roles of the producers in *Ma Rainey's Black Bottom*, then you're altering one of the main themes of the play, the oppression and institutional racism faced by African American artists in the early twentieth century. Non-traditional casting can come in many forms—whether it's through gender-flipping, age, nationality, or what have you—but the important thing to remember is that it needs to have *some* kind of logic behind it. As long as you are casting to fit the needs of *your* production, then you'll be on the right track.

Are you casting based on compatibility? MacArthur Award-winning director and choreographer Martha Clarke says that she "need[s] a

69

commitment like a love affair with my cast ... The work is very intimate, very process-oriented ... I really want their souls—not after five o'clock, but when they're in the studio."[1] While she is obviously not talking about a romantic relationship with all of her company members, Ms Clarke's quote illustrates the level of importance compatibility holds. Whether you are looking to cast actors who are compatible with one another or who are compatible with you, if this is your primary criterion then it will be vital to find the right fit. Compatibility will always come into play at some level—you want to have a cast who are responsive to your vision as a director and to each other as artists—but whether or not you want it to be the driving influence behind your decisions will depend on your needs for a given production. You may find that an intimate show, with only a few cast members—like John Logan's *Red* or Yazmina Reza's *God of Carnage*—puts more of a premium on compatibility between the actors than large-scale shows like Lerner and Loewe's *My Fair Lady* or Kaufman and Hart's *You Can't Take it With You*. The importance of compatibility between director and actor oftentimes depends on subject matter more than cast size, with something like Doug Wright's *I Am My Own Wife* requiring much more compatibility between director and performer than a play like Jack Holmes' *RFK*, despite both being one-person shows.

Are you casting based on specific needs? As mentioned above, some roles require that an actor be a specific race, gender, age, ethnicity, or nationality, based either on the way they were written or because of the concept you have selected for your production. Other roles may have certain requirements for actors that revolve around specific talents or skillsets. Examples include singing, dancing, stage combat, juggling, dialects, puppetry, roller skating, etc. There may also be certain things required of an actor playing a role that might limit your options when it comes to casting. Nudity, swearing, intimate contact, smoking, and drinking are a few examples of these. Still other roles may simply be ones that some actors may not want to play (rapists, murderers, etc.).

Some of these skills, talents, and character traits may show up in auditions, but for some you may have to see what an actor has on his or her résumé, or wait until the callback to find out what you need. A big key to making sure you have an easy path in casting is to make sure that you provide actors with as much information up front as you can. Whether in the breakdown, audition announcement, pre-audition press, or comments to the actors who come to audition, let them know ahead of time what to expect. If you're directing *The Grapes of Wrath*, then you need to make sure that any actresses auditioning for Rose of Sharon know ahead of time that the role requires them to breastfeed a dying man onstage. That knowledge ahead of time can eliminate some actresses who might not be comfortable with that type of exposure. Also, it saves you the trouble of being two weeks into rehearsal and having an actress say "Ummmm ... I don't think I can do that." If you haven't asked actors auditioning to prepare a song, or be ready for a dance call, or to perform a monologue in a dialect, then you will need to pay particular attention to the skills and previous shows they have listed on their résumés. Don't, however, rely strictly on what they have written down. When it comes down to it, make sure you see what you need to see in callbacks.

Are there any other elements that might affect your casting? In addition to the questions discussed here, you need to make sure that you are aware of anything else that might affect your casting, before you head into auditions. Though this is by no means an exhaustive list, here are a few considerations:

- Know your talent pool. Are you going to be able to cast your show with the local talent you have available, or will you have to go outside of your area?
- Know your budget. Is there a budget line for actor salaries? If so, what is it and how is it divided up between the various roles?
- Know your theatre's contract. Are you working at a non-union house? If so, unless your producer has a guest-artist contract, your friend who's a member of Equity won't have a spot in your show.

After you've answered the questions about how you plan on casting your show, you need to go through your script and list your ideal actor for each role. When listing your ideal actor, you should use a combination of descriptions and suggestions. The descriptions should be adjectives that describe your ideal actor for that role. Make sure that your description list takes into account appearance, vocal quality, and personality. Don't forget to include any special skills that the role might require. In addition to the list of descriptions, it is often helpful to make a suggestion of a specific actor who would fit this role. For this, you can use famous actors, or actors who are only known to you. Try to avoid, however, suggesting actors within your current talent pool (those who you know will be auditioning for your show). If you include those, you may find yourself pre-casting the show accidentally.

A word, finally, about pre-casting. Many professional theatres will pre-cast some or all of their roles before auditions begin. In fact, you may often be hired to direct a show and have the leads cast ahead of time, so your casting will focus on the other characters. Regional theatres and higher may cast principal roles, and use an Equity open call to fill in the rest. Educational, community, and church theatres, however, typically will not pre-cast a show. Regardless of the policy at the theatre where you direct, make sure that it is known ahead of time to all of the actors coming to audition. Auditioning is a tough process, as anyone who has ever acted can tell you. The one thing that actors must know going into an audition is that they will get a fair shot. There's no quicker way to lose the trust of local actors (and thus shrink your available talent pool) than to hold auditions for roles you already have cast, but haven't told anyone about. Remember, you want every actor who comes to auditions to do well, because the best problem you can have as a director is having too many great choices.

72

During Auditions

Here we come to the single most important rule about casting: *cast on the audition*. If Actor A gives a horrible audition, then Actor B gives a terrific audition, you cannot cast Actor A based on the idea, "Well, he just had a bad night. I know he can do better." A former colleague had a sign on her office wall that said:

Life is not fair.
Theatre is less fair than life.
Acting is the least fair part of theatre.
Human beings submit themselves to nothing less fair than the audition.

The audition process, as we know, is inherently unfair and is not necessarily a meritocracy. It is therefore incumbent upon the director to make the process as fair and equitable as possible. To do so, you *must* cast on what you see in the audition. Yes, the possibility does exist that you will get burned by this approach. There are some actors who are absolutely fantastic at auditions, but that is the zenith of their performance capabilities. Fortunately, that is not the case for most actors, and you will find that the audition is just a jumping off point for them.

Casting on the audition does not mean, however, that you should completely discount previous experiences with an actor. If you have worked with an actor before and know that he or she is troublesome (and that word can really cover a broad range of problems), you may choose not to work with that actor again, regardless of the strength of the audition. While this can be a perfectly legitimate reason not to cast someone, you have to be careful that it doesn't devolve into a decision based purely on personality differences. Remember that your goal is to help create the best show possible. There's a difference between not casting actors because they are a disruptive influence or won't take direction and not casting them because you just don't like them very much.

As you get into the actual auditions themselves, keep your list of ideals that you created prior to auditions in mind for each character. Also, realize that you are *never* going to get your ideals. "Why," you may be asking, "should I make a list of ideals if I'm not going to get to cast them?" Excellent question, you perspicacious reader! You create the list of ideals so you know who you would cast in a "perfect world," but you approach the actual auditions using that list as a guide. You will want to cast as close to your ideal for each character as you can, and having the list makes comparisons easier. Be open-minded when watching the auditions and remember that you are looking for *possibilities* for each role. There are two mind-sets to watching auditions: character-centric and actor-centric. One approach is not necessarily better than the other; it really comes down to which works best for you.

The character-centric approach to auditions means that you are going to be focusing on the needs of the characters as you watch the auditions. When setting up to take your audition notes, you will want to keep in mind the ideal descriptions you came up with for each character so that you can then match the actors to the characters for which they will be considered (see Figure 5.1).

As you can see from the example, you'll want to have a list of the characters in the show, with your ideal descriptors next to each character's name. As actors take the stage, you immediately have to decide the character(s) for which you wish to consider them. The drawback to this approach is that you are making snap decisions that may cause you to leave actors out of consideration for other roles they could fit in the show. The benefit of this quick-assessment

Character	Ideal	Actor/Notes	Actor/Notes	Actor/Notes	Actor/Notes
Macbeth	Strong. Long hair. Physically imposing. Over 6 feet. Needs to fight and dance. Built like an athlete	Mark (#1)/Good monologue. Tall. Needs to command the stage better. Awfully thin.	Ryan (#23)/Perfect height and build. Deep voice. Good presence. Didn't handle the language great.	Jake (#27)/Shorter than need. Excellent monologue. Great command of the language. Moves really well. Bald.	Steve (#46)/Big guy—tall and heavy. Good vocal work. Glad to see him move in the monologue. Looks like a former soccer player.
Lady Macbeth	Calculating. Scheming. Physically imposing. Over 5'7". Needs to look good paired with Macbeth. Red hair. Needs to be a dancer and built like an athlete.	Stacy (#3)/Angular face. Black hair (could we dye it?). Good slate and vocals. Not sure she understood her monologue completely. Needs to be in better control.	Mary (#16)/Definitely a dancer. A little on the short side. Good monologue choice to show her scheming attitude. Great vocal work. Blonde hair.	Katie (#22)/Taaallll. Taller than any of our potential Macbeths. Really high-pitched voice. Looks like a basketball or volleyball player. Redhead.	Jamey (#51)/Great look—perfect fit against any of the MacB possibilities. Vocals need a lot of work. Need to see if she can be manipulative.

Figure 5.1 An example of character-centric audition notes.

approach is that it forces you immediately to look at every actor in terms of what character they could play, from the moment they set foot on the stage.

If you decide to use an actor-centric approach to note taking during your auditions, you will be focusing more directly on the actor. When preparing to take your notes in this fashion, you will want to make sure you identify the actor by name, number, and, in your notes, a description. Yes, you'll have headshots to jog your memory, but seeing your own thoughts as you wrote them down will really help you connect. Additionally, you'll want to make sure that you list the possibilities you see for the actor in the show (see Figure 5.2).

The example only shows a few of the auditionees; obviously, there would be a row for each person who auditions. The biggest benefit to viewing auditions through this prism is that you are really able to focus on actors and the audition, from the moment that they walk on the stage. A concern for this method, however, is that you have to make sure you don't get so wrapped up in watching the audition that you forget to think about what the actor is doing in relation to the show or the character possibilities.

Ultimately, *possibilities* are what you are looking for when you are watching auditions. If you have the opportunity to hold callbacks, then you are looking for several possibilities that you can call back and see in more detail. If, however, you are not holding callbacks, then you will be looking at as many possible actors for each role as you can find. Remember that your goal when casting the show is to come as close to the ideal for each character as you can. With that

74

Number	Actor	Notes	Possibilities
1	Mark	Tall guy. Very thin. Really good monologue choice. Nice shape to it. Didn't command the space very well—particularly on his entrance. Needs to finish the piece stronger.	Macbeth, Banquo, Siward, Donalbain (maybe?)
3	Stacy	Really sharp features. Would that black hair dye to red, or would we have to wig her? Good personality and vocals on slate. Needs to make more sense of the monologue... just a lot of words right now. Control your breathing more.	Lady Macbeth, Witch #2 Lady Macduff
16	Mary	Total dancer-look. Might be shorter than what we'd like for Lady Mac. Nice choice of monologue—really shows off her scheming. Strong vocal work throughout the piece. Good to see her understanding of scansion. Blonde hair—could definitely go red with no problem.	Lady Macbeth, Witch #1
22	Katie	REALLY tall. Probably taller than any Macbeth we might cast. Voice is way up in her upper register. Upper thoracic breathing. Need to sink breathing and play with pitch variety more. Looks like she probably was (or is) an athlete—basketball or volleyball. Red hair.	Lady Macbeth
23	Ryan	Perfect look for MacB. Just the right height and build—looks like a tight end from the football team. Strong presence from the moment he walked onstage for his slate. Didn't handle the language in the best fashion. Needs to make the connection between thought and word more, and make it more organic.	Macbeth, Macduff, Duncan
27	Jake	Probably too short for MacB. Great monologue, though. Commanded the language really well and showed his movement training in the piece. Definitely looks like he could fight and dance. Bald head.	Macbeth, Banquo, Malcolm
46	Steve	Big fella. Well over 6 feet (6'6" or 6'7") and probably close to 300 lbs. Instant command of the stage. Surprisingly sweet persona on slate. Vocal work was good throughout. Understood the text and played with his voice effectively. Moved better than expected. With his size, he could have been a goal keeper.	Macbeth, Duncan, Macduff
51	Jamey	Great look for Lady Mac. Would probably fit well with any of the MacB possibilities—just the right height and build. Didn't come across as very confident in her slate. Vocal work in the monologue was weak. Volume and breath control problems are tough for her. Wish she'd chosen a better monologue to show a manipulative side.	Lady Macbeth, Witch #3

Figure 5.2 An example of actor-centric audition notes.

thought in the forefront of your mind, you will begin to see the show take shape in your head as you are watching the auditions.

Post-Auditions

With the auditions finished, the actual casting process begins. For some directors, this is the most torturous part of the entire production, while for others, this is their favorite part. For those who find this difficult, it is often because they don't want to hurt anyone's feelings, or they've seen so many good auditions they feel they can't make a choice. Remember that you're trying to cast the best actors for *your* production. Whether or not you cast someone isn't a judgment on the actor as a person—it's choosing the best fit for each role. Try not to personalize the process too much, even if you are friends with some of the actors who auditioned. The fact of the matter is, there will always be disappointed actors when the casting is over. The best ones, the ones you want to work with now or in the future, will not let the disappointment make them bitter or angry. They learn and grow from each audition and will be back to showcase their talents for you on the next production.

The first thing to remember about sitting in the casting room—whether you are a director, an assistant director, a stage manager, or a production assistant—is that anything that is said about an actor in that room *does not leave that room*. Casting, by its very nature, involves critiquing performances, looks, and personality. It should always be professional in nature and never take a personal turn, but even so, you never want an actor to hear through the grapevine that you said: "John looks awfully short and frumpy when he stands next to Kelly. I don't know if he would look right in the role." After going through and organizing the audition forms, headshots, résumés, and your notes, you can begin the four-step process of casting: 1 eliminate the non-starters; 2 decide on the definites; 3 explore the possibilities; 4 make the cuts.

Eliminate the Non-Starters

Typically, the casting room for any show I direct becomes a sea of paperwork, as I divide the audition forms, résumés, and headshots into stacks. The first stack is always the "non-starter" stack. These are the actors that I know, right from the beginning, that I will not be casting in the show. Some of them I realized when I first saw them in the audition room, whereas with others I gradually came to the conclusion that I will not be able to cast them. The reasons for not casting them could be as varied as the actors themselves, and are unimportant to the process. This step is really just to "clear the decks" so you can get to work with all the actors you might possibly use. It is always a good idea, though, to make sure that you, your stage management team, or someone in the company keeps up with the audition materials of this (and every other) group. You never know when you might be embarking on another show for which a previously uncast actor could be perfect this time around.

Decide on the Definites

These first two steps are usually the simplest parts of the casting process. Most auditions (hopefully) have at least one actor who leaps out at you during the process, and you know right away that you are going to cast that person (or maybe, persons). Once you've eliminated the non-starters, you then pull out the ones you know absolutely that you will cast, and begin creating the stack of forms that will eventually comprise the cast for your show. If you're *really* lucky, the best choices for each and every role will have shown themselves in the auditions/callbacks, and your job will be done here; though, in over two decades of directing, I have never been that lucky! More likely, you will find one or two of the actors you need in this step, and then be ready to move on to the next one.

Explore the Possibilities

Oftentimes, once you cast one or more of the principal characters, other roles tend to fall into place because you are casting based on how everyone looks in relation to (or the chemistry they have with) that principal actor. For example, if you are able to determine that Anna is your Juliet, your decisions for Lord and Lady Capulet, the Nurse, Romeo, and Tybalt become easier, because you're looking for actors who pair well with Anna. It may be, however, that you have more than one actor who could pair up well with Anna. Or it may be that you have an actor who could pair well with Anna as *either* Romeo *or* Tybalt. This is the part of the casting process that begins to get difficult. At this point, you will be looking at two sets of possibilities: Which actors could play this role? And … Which roles could this actor play? To continue with our *Romeo and Juliet* example, you will find yourself creating stacks that have two or three possible Romeos, one or two possible Nurses, four or five possible Lord Capulets, etc. You may decide that some actors go in more than one stack (i.e. the example above, where the actor could be cast either as Romeo or Tybalt). This is where the criteria you established for yourself prior to beginning auditions really becomes valuable. The casting process can often become tumultuous, especially if there are a lot of voices in the room. It can become easy, when choosing between possibilities, to be swayed by the tiniest of details (or the loudest voice). If you make sure to stick to the criteria you set for your show prior to auditions, then you will find yourself able to choose much more easily.

77

Make the Cuts

Hopefully, by the time you finish with Step 3, you will have the vast majority of your show cast. (The word "cast" works in both future and past tense: "casted" is *never* appropriate. Should you find yourself saying "Sally was casted in the show," I will have to jump through the pages of this book and roundly chastise you.) Inevitably, though, there will be a role or two that are particularly difficult to fill. You will often find that you have two (sometimes more) actors who are almost equal in all respects. They each had great auditions, they both look good for the part, they can both perform any special tasks you need, and both have the same level of training. In instances like this, it is best to "flip the script" as you finish casting. Instead of looking for the best person for the role, you will need to look for reasons *not* to cast one of the actors. When everything else is equal, you have to start searching for a reason to cut an actor from your list. It may be that Actor A has blonde hair and Actor B has brown hair and you don't have the budget to dye hair, so you cut Actor B. Perhaps Actor A is 6'1" and Actor B is 6'3" and the tallest actor in the rest of the cast is 5'11", so you cut Actor B because you don't want him to stand out too much. As you can see, the final decision-making process really can get nit-picky. Eventually, though, you will be able to work your way through your list and (hopefully) have a cast that will work wonders for your show.

The magnificent Peter Brook has said that

[a] role is a meeting, a meeting between an actor as a mass of potentialities—and a catalyst. Because a role is a form of catalyst ... when it encounters the human material which is the individual actor, [it] creates all the time new specifics.[2]

The infinite possibilities presented by different actors provide each role, then, with an infinite possibility of performances. Your work when casting the show will connect the actor with the catalyst of the role. With proper planning and good fortune, the resulting performance will be perfect for your production. Remember, however, that you are casting *one* actor in a role. Too often, directors who have difficulty making casting decisions because they don't want to hurt anyone's feelings will decide that the answer to their decision-making problem lies in selecting multiple versions of the cast, an "A cast" and a "B cast," if you will. Unless you went into the process with the knowledge that you were going to cast understudies (and your budget allows it), that is not something you want to decide on at the last minute. The extra rehearsals, performance decisions, and personalities that come with that choice almost always wind up causing more trouble than anyone wants to deal with in a production. Another way I have seen some directors deal with difficult choices is to put an actor in another role in the show. The thinking goes like this: "OK, I have Suzie and Carmen as possibilities for Eliza Doolittle. I'm going to cast Carmen, but we'll put Suzie in the ensemble, because she's so good, I'd hate to not cast her." No! If you haven't begun the process of casting with a particular role in mind (in this case, going into it considering Suzie for an ensemble role), then you don't want to randomly shove an actor into a role "just because." Remember, there are no consolation prizes in casting.

A final word about this whole process, then. As we've said throughout the book, you are the ultimate leader of the production's merry band. The show is your vision and you are the one casting the deciding vote. As such, you need to make sure you take responsibility for your casting decisions. When actors have a question about why they did or did not get cast in the role they wanted, you are the one who has to answer. Many actors, looking to improve their auditioning skills, will ask what they can work on in order to do better the next time around. Answer them honestly and helpfully because, remember, you want the actors to do well. Also, if there is a complaint about the casting, you are the one to deal with that complaint—even if the choice was, in some way, not yours (more often than not, this only happens in educational and community theatre). I once directed a musical and had the option of two different actors for one of the principal roles. Because the actors were so evenly matched, I asked the choreographer about "Actor A," and her ability to perform the choreography the role required. The choreographer immediately told me that she would not be able to handle it, so we cast "Actor B." Because that was a role that Actor A really, *really* wanted, she was most unhappy with me for not casting her. The next day, after the cast list had gone out, the choreographer came to me and said, "You know, I was thinking about the wrong role. Actor A could have done this one just fine." Needless to say, I wasn't thrilled to hear that, but the decisions had been made and the cast list had gone out. While it might have been easy to shift the blame to the choreographer when Actor A came to complain (and she did), as the director I had to take ownership of the decisions made. While my friendship with the actor suffered a bit, the needs of the show added that extra level of responsibility. Take ownership of your production, and remember: if you want the fun, excitement, and creative license of being a director, you have to take the proverbial good with the bad in all areas.

Exercises and Suggested Reading

Exercises

1. Using *The Glass Menagerie* (or another play, as chosen by your instructor) as a case study, list your ideal cast. Make sure to include a description and a person for each character. Share your list with your class. Be prepared to explain why you made the choices you did, and to discuss differences in ideal casting between you and your classmates.
2. Using the same show from the first exercise, partner with an acting class to conduct mock auditions. Half the class should focus on taking character-centric notes during the auditions and half should take actor-centric notes. After the mock auditions, compare your impressions with your classmates.
3. Again, using the same show and the mock auditions you've watched, "cast" the production. Go through the four-step process to come up with your cast. Share your cast with the class, and be prepared to discuss why you did (or did not) cast each actor who "auditioned."

Notes

1. Arthur Bartow, *The Director's Voice* (New York: Theatre Communications Group, 1988), 60.
2. Peter Brook, *The Shifting Point* (New York: Harper & Row, 1987), 221–222.

Suggested Reading

Galati, Frank. *The Grapes of Wrath* (New York: Dramatists Play Service, 1991).

Hauptmann, William (book) and Miller, Roger (music and lyrics). *Big River* (New York: Rodgers and Hammerstein Library, 2003 (1985)).

Henley, Beth. *The Miss Firecracker Contest* (New York: Dramatists Play Service, 1998 (1979)).

Holmes, Jack. *RFK* (New York: Dramatists Play Service, 2009).

Kaufman, George S. and Hart, Moss. *You Can't Take It With You* (New York: Dramatists Play Service, 1998 (1937)).

Lerner, Alan (book and lyrics) and Loewe, Frederick (music). *My Fair Lady* (New York: Tams-Witmark, 1962 (1959)).

Logan, John. *Red* (New York: Dramatists Play Service, 2011 (2009)).

Meehan, Thomas (book), Flaherty, Stephen, and Ahrens, Lynn (music and lyrics). *Rocky the Musical.* Currently available as Original Cast Recording (Santa Monica, CA: Hip-O Records, 2014).

Reza, Yazmina. *God of Carnage* (New York: Dramatists Play Service, 2009 (2006)).

Silver, Nicky. *Fat Men in Skirts* (New York: Dramatists Play Service, 1994 (1988)).

Shakespeare, William. *A Midsummer Night's Dream* (c.1590–1597, available online).

Shakespeare, William. *Othello* (1603, available online).

Sheik, Duncan (music) and Sater, Steven (book and lyrics). *Spring Awakening* (New York: Samuel French, 2007).

Sondheim, Stephen (music and lyrics) and Wheeler, Hugh (book). *Sweeney Todd* (Milwaukee, WI: Applause Musical Library, 2000 (1979)).

Stewart, Michael (book), Adams, Lee (lyrics), and Strauss, Charles (music). *Bye, Bye, Birdie* (New York: Tams-Witmark, 1958).

Williams, Tennessee. *The Glass Menagerie* (New York: Dramatists Play Service, 1998 (1944)).

Wilson, August. *Ma Rainey's Black Bottom* (New York: Plume, 1985 (1981)).

Wright, Doug. *I Am My Own Wife* (New York: Dramatists Play Service, 2005 (1992)).

CHAPTER 6

Technology and Social Media

You've prepared, researched, auditioned, and cast your show. Before we turn our discussion to rehearsals, though, let's talk about use of technology as a director. We won't be covering utilization of technology as *part* of a performance (that's another book entirely), but instead we'll look at how you can use technology in service to your production. I should state up front that, with the pace of change in all technological fields, some of the things I mention in this chapter may change or cease to exist by the time you read this. I'll do my best to refer to generally open-source/free services. While you may not be able to make use of some of the specific sites or programs I mention, there are plenty out there that serve the same function. For our purposes, the technology we'll look at falls into three categories: production organization; communication and contact; and promotions and marketing. Some of the ideas, suggestions, and programs overlap categories, but we will try to separate them out as best we can. All of these are simple to use, however, and none requires a degree in computer technology!

Production Organization

Though nothing will ever take the place of in-person production meetings, the reality is that all of our lives move at a faster pace and we all like the convenience and flexibility of working electronically. Perhaps you've seen the little ribbons that say, "I successfully survived another meeting that could have been handled with an email." There are certainly times when those in-person meetings drag on and on and can severely cut into your work day. While email is a great way to keep in daily contact, it doesn't always provide immediate responses, nor does it allow for efficient collaboration between everyone on the production team. Because of that, there are certain resources you can use that allow freedom of contact and collaboration. Document-sharing services like Google Drive and Dropbox, Facebook groups, and dedicated websites are just a few of the options you have when it comes to production organization.

Document Sharing

Document-sharing sites and services, like Google Drive and Dropbox, are excellent tools for your production team. With them, you and your collaborators can devise and share all the research and forms that everyone needs access to throughout a production. With the ability to create and edit folders, it's easy to organize and keep track of everything. Typically, for each show I direct, I will create a master folder for the production. Once you do that, you should make sure that you set it up so that all collaborators have editing capabilities in the folder. That way, they are able to add items, edit, and comment.

If you look at Figure 6.1 (the redacted portions are people's names), you'll find an image of a Google Drive folder we used at Louisiana Tech University for a production of Alfred Uhry's *The Last Night of Ballyhoo*. You see that the master folder contains things such as rehearsal schedules and costume plots, as well as sub-folders, including one for director's notes, stage management, research, and sound design. All members of the production team were shared on the folder, allowing them access and the ability to create, add, and edit.

Figure 6.1 A sample of a shared Google Drive folder.

Figure 6.2 shows the Research sub-folder that we used for *Bally-hoo*. In this folder, the director, AD, designers, and dramaturg were all able to upload and share their research. With that folder accessible to everyone, any time a question arose, it was able to be answered quickly. Want to know why the scenic designer made specific choices for window locations? You have that information at your fingertips. And it's a lot quicker (and easier) than waiting for a reply to an email.

The next folder, seen in Figure 6.3, was created by the show's production stage manager. Within this folder, the PSM was able to organize all reports, forms, and lists that are the lifeblood of every production. The beauty of document sharing is that everything is in a centralized location, and if you label everything carefully, anyone needing to step in for any reason (or a producer who wants to keep track of things) can do so easily and find everything that is needed.

Finally, in Figure 6.4, you see the sub-folder for the director's notes. Organizing your notes in this fashion has more than one benefit. Because it is in "the cloud," and not kept on a flash drive or

Figure 6.2 The "research" sub-folder.

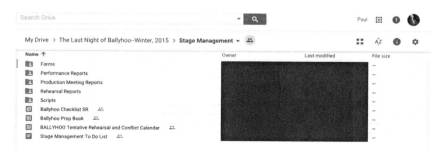

Figure 6.3 The "stage management" sub-folder.

Search Drive | Paul

My Drive > The Last Night of Ballyhoo--Winter, 2015 > Director's Notes ▾

Name ↑	Owner	Last modified	File size
1/5/15 Off Book Act I	me	Jan 6, 2015 me	--
1/6/15 Off Book Act II	me	Jan 6, 2015 me	--
1st Dress	me	Jan 26, 2015 me	--
AD Notes_ 1-09-15.docx	me	Jan 12, 2015 me	19 KB
AD Notes_ 1-09-15.docx	me	Jan 13, 2015 me	--
AD Notes_1-08-15.docx	me	Jan 12, 2015 me	19 KB
AUDITIONS 12/8/14	me	Dec 8, 2014 me	--
Ballyhoo Photo Call List	me	Feb 5, 2015 me	--
Callbacks	me	Dec 9, 2014 me	--
Director's Notes for Program	me	Jan 22, 2015 me	--
FINAL DRESS	me	Jan 27, 2015 me	--
January 14 Runthru	me	Jan 14, 2015 me	--
January 15 RunThru	me	Jan 15, 2015 me	--
January 16 RunThru	me	Jan 17, 2015 me	--
January 20	me	Jan 20, 2015 me	--
January 21	me	Jan 21, 2015 me	--
January 23	me	Jan 23, 2015 me	--
Notes on AD	me	Jan 13, 2015 me	--
Tech-Dress	me	Jan 25, 2015 me	--

Figure 6.4 The "director's notes" sub-folder.

hard drive, your notes are easily located and accessed, no matter where you are. Have you decided to meet with cast members at a coffee shop on a Saturday afternoon to give notes from Friday's rehearsal? If you bring your phone, you can access everything you need. Additionally, because the documents are shared, other members of the production team can read and reply to the notes in real time. In Figure 6.4, if you notice the document labeled "tech-dress," designers were able to have that document open during the rehearsal to see my notes as I was typing them. If, say, a note about a step that needed painting was already known and noted by the technical director, he was able to type a quick "on it" under my note. The efficiency of collaboration is improved drastically with these services.

Facebook Groups

Creating a "closed" Facebook group is another way that your production team can share and keep up with information. Other social media platforms could also serve the same purpose (i.e. Pinterest, Tumblr, etc.), but Facebook is relatively ubiquitous and simple to use. The most important key to remember if you are going to use Facebook as your electronic collaboration repository, is the privacy setting.

Note that you are given three options: "open," "closed," and "secret." You will want to make sure that you select "secret." By

85

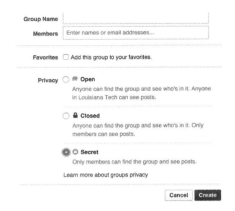

Figure 6.5 Privacy settings.

doing that, you will assure that no one could accidentally stumble on your page and access it.

Once you have created your group, you will have most of the same options available to you as with the document-sharing services. The biggest difference is that you really won't have a viable way to share *actual* documents. Facebook is great for passing along messages and notes, sharing photos, videos, sound, and scheduling. However, unlike document-sharing sites, you won't be able to upload notes or comments and you won't have the ability to create and annotate in "real time." It is much better suited as a central location to store show-related information.

Dedicated Websites

There are a host of "build your own website" services available online for free (if you are willing to put up with the ads). Like Facebook, though, these sites are much more conducive to sharing information, and don't provide the opportunity for real-time collaboration. Unlike Facebook, however, most of these sites either allow for documents to be uploaded, or they can be created within the framework of the site. There are two things to remember when working with these sites, though: first, each member of your production team will need to be set as an administrator (which allows them access to upload material); second, when uploading documents to one of these online website creators it is best to do so in pdf format, as typical word-processing formats are often not recognized and your document can become garbled.

No matter what method you use for your production organization, always bear in mind the issue of privacy. Remember that anything created in the cloud or shared online, regardless of privacy setting, has the potential to be found or hacked by others. Make sure you are following your theatre's privacy policy before putting any truly sensitive information out there.

Communication and Contact

Communication and contact with your company is, perhaps, the most important aspect about a production that doesn't directly deal with the production itself. Call times for rehearsals, fittings, promotional and photo calls, and schedule changes are a daily part of the production process. While, in most theatres, it will be the production stage manager who is responsible for maintaining day-to-day contact with the company, as the director you need to make sure you are aware of the process and how it works. Remember, as we've said before, many of you will start out working on projects where you find yourself as the director, PSM, and light board op, all rolled into one. With that in mind, think about the various options you have to keep open the lines of communication with your company. Gone, thankfully, are the days of the stage management team having to make 35 individual phonecalls to let actors and designers know that a rehearsal has been rescheduled; instead, there are now a variety of electronic means that make communication quick and efficient. Three of the best ways to keep in contact with your company are "virtual callboards," Twitter, and electronic messaging.

Virtual Callboards

The term "virtual callboard" is a generic phrase that refers to any web-based message board. These can take the form of closed Facebook groups or DIY websites (as mentioned in the previous section), or they could be integrated as part of your theatre company's official website. Functioning in exactly the same way that a traditional, "physical" callboard does, VCs allow you to post and edit all information that might be relevant to your company. At Louisiana Tech University, our VC is divided into five categories: "rehearsal and work calls," "announcements," "calendar," "resources," and "directory." As with any physical callboard you might find in a college theatre department, we post as much relevant information for our students as we can.

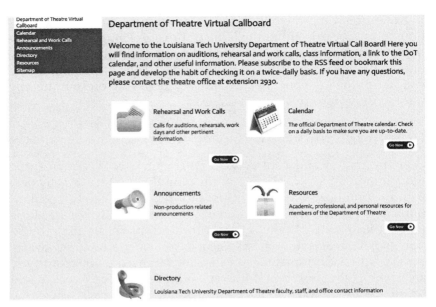

Figure 6.6 Screenshot of the Louisiana Tech Department of Theatre virtual callboard.

There are two things of which you should be aware, should you decide to use a VC for your company. First, it is an *active* communication method (the other two, which we will get to in a minute, are *passive* communication tools), which means that your actors and crew have to make the choice to visit the website each day (often multiple times) to check whether there are any new posts. We recommend to our students that they set the VC as their browser's homepage, so it is the first thing they see whenever they open it up— whether on a computer, tablet, or phone. Alternatively, company members can subscribe to the RSS feed and receive a notification when the site is updated. In either case, it requires them to visit the site on their own. The second thing to remember, when using a VC, is that it absolutely must be kept current, if you want people to rely on it. Since most of us are used to consuming information online, we expect the websites we visit to be "up to the minute" with their information; this absolutely applies to your VC as well. If members of your company do as they are asked and check the site regularly but fail to find the most current information, they will quickly get out of the habit.

Twitter

While Twitter can require active communication, it can be set up to serve in the passive model as well. Creating an account for your company's administrative use is simple and free. Once you have created your account, you'll have to make sure that each member of your company: (a) has a Twitter account; and (b) follows the administrative account you've activated. To ensure that company members never miss an important tweet, instruct everyone to go into their settings once they follow your account, and select "turn on mobile notifications." Once they have done this, any tweet you send out will be sent to their phones as a text message. The benefit of using Twitter in this manner is that actors and crew can tweet questions to the account if they are unsure of a call-time or other important information. Of course, this means that someone will need to monitor the account to answer any questions your company might have.

Electronic Messaging

Text messaging is almost ubiquitous in the United States these days, and provides another passive means (for your company members) of staying in contact. As of 2014, according to a Pew Research Center project, 81 percent of cell phone owners use their phones to send or receive text messages.[1] Sending text messages to your company members is most likely the quickest and most efficient method of communicating with them, as so many people stay constantly connected with their phones. Many phone types allow you to create text message groups, so that you can message everyone at once. A major drawback of that method, though, is that when people reply—with a question, comment, or response—the messages can get garbled as to who is sending and/or replying ... and for whom they are intended. Take a look at Figure 6.7 for an example of a group text message.

In the example, you see a rehearsal call-time sent, with four responses. The last responder needs clarification, and the PSM replies with a new call-time. You can see how, rather easily, some actors, opening their phones and scanning the list of messages, might see that last one and assume that 3:00 is the new call-time for everyone.

To avoid that type of confusion, group messaging apps that provide one-way communication can be used. Most of these applications require users to have a smartphone, though those devices are more and more common in the US. The Pew Research Center's 2015 report on smartphone usage noted that almost two-thirds of US citizens owned smartphones as of spring 2015.[2] "Remind" is an app

Figure 6.7 A confusing group text message.

that is popular among teachers as a way to communicate quickly with students and parents. Allowing for one-way messaging (meaning that the recipients cannot reply within the app's message), applications like this allow you to send a message to your company that can be set to be received as a text message, email, or push notification. Since the message is only one-way, there is no risk of confusion. Most of these apps also allow for individual chats to be established between users, so questions and answers don't go to the entire group.

Whatever method you use to communicate with your company, make sure that you are doing so efficiently, regularly, and clearly, so that you don't leave any room for misunderstanding. There is nothing quite so frustrating as having an entire company standing around and waiting for one actor who is late to rehearsal because he didn't receive or understand the call.

Promotions and Marketing

Promotions and marketing will be the area covered in this chapter that you, as a director, will most likely deal with least. In most larger companies, in fact, the director might have nothing to do with promotions and marketing, beyond making promotional appearances to talk about the show. However, for those of you working in smaller professional theatres, educational theatres, church theatres, and community theatres, you may very well have a much more active part in this area. While nothing takes the place of a full-time promotions and marketing department, and if you haven't been trained in the field you won't be as successful as those who have, there are certain things you can do to aid in your company's promotional efforts. For our purposes, we will briefly look at websites, social media, and broadcasting as relatively simple means you can employ to aid your company's promotions and marketing, should you be called upon to do so.

Websites

As we've mentioned in the previous two sections of this chapter, there are plenty of DIY programs out there that make it easy for just about anyone to create a website. Using drag and drop for photos and templates for text, most of these can be up and running (and look quite good) in a single day. If you are going to create a site to promote your company, there are a few things you can do to make it more effective:

1. Grab your audience's attention quickly. According to the Nielson Norman Group, people surfing online for content "often leave Web pages in 10–20 seconds, but pages with a clear value proposition can hold people's attention for much longer."[3] How can you offer people a "clear value proposition?" Using colors and contrast makes your page visually appealing and increases the chance that people will stay on your site longer.

2. Keep your audience interested. Once you have the audience on your website, don't let them get bored with your content. Photos and images to break up text blocks keep your page stimulating and keep the viewer from zoning out. Try to avoid long blocks of text or description. Use short, attention-grabbing phrases, and keep your audience involved.

3. Give your audience useful information. No matter if you are a professional company, educational theatre, church theatre, or community theatre, your audience is going to visit your page for one reason above all others: to find information about your next show. Make sure that performance (and box office) information is easy to find and clear to understand.

4. Make it mobile! More and more people are accessing websites via tablets or smartphones. Whichever site-building service you choose, make sure that it will be clear, clean, quick, and legible when viewed in a mobile format.

Social Media

Your theatre company's social media presence is going to be your primary means of communication with the vast majority of your audience members. Facebook, Twitter, Instagram, Pinterest, Snapchat, YouTube, and other such sites are invaluable for the day-to-day promotion of your company and individual productions. Identifying which social media outlets your audiences use most often will be key to your efforts. If you don't have access to local market research data, you can conduct unofficial surveys among the audiences of your shows. If three-quarters of your audience use Instagram, but not Twitter, that will be beneficial for you to know. There are three important things to remember when using social media as part of your promotions and marketing:

1. Keep it active. How many times a day do you check your various social media feeds? 5? 10? 20? More? And when you do check them, do you expect to see the same content each time? Of course not. And how many times a day to you post on your own social media profiles? When you are posting on your company's site, remember that people are checking in and out all day long and they like to see new content, at the very least, every day.
2. Keep it interesting. Short blurbs, quick videos, "behind the scenes" photographs ... these are the kinds of things that catch the eye and interest potential audience members. A chance to pull back the curtain on a show and see a 60-second video interview with one of your actors is a great way to bring your audience in and interest them in your show.
3. Keep it on task. The social media company, Hootsuite, talks about the importance of having a social media content calendar: "A social media calendar cuts extra time out of your content marketing strategy and helps you allocate your resources wisely, to help ensure your brand consistently publishes high-quality, well-written, high-performing content pieces."[4] You can utilize the content calendar to make sure you know what, where, and when you are posting. If more

than one person has access to your social media accounts (as is often the case in educational theatres, where faculty and students post content), this is particularly helpful at getting everyone to stay on task.

Broadcasting

Broadcasting, for lack of a better term, is another way to "pull back the curtain" for your audience. Rehearsal clips, backstage tours, cast interviews, or even short tutorials can be used to engage your audience. And ultimately, engaging your audience is what this is all about. You want to make a connection with your audience *prior* to their coming to the theatre. You need to entice them to come see the show, and helping them feel like an "insider" is one of the best ways to do this. There are various means at your disposal to accomplish this, from simple to complex:

1. *Audio*. Soundcloud, Bandcamp, and Audioboo are just three of the popular websites that allow a user to upload and mix sound. This is great if you want to record a vocal run-through of a number in a musical you're directing, or a brief commentary from you or one of the designers. The sites also allow you to embed what you record on your own website, so it makes it easy for your audience to listen.

2. *Video*. YouTube and Vimeo are the most popular sites for user-generated content, and both can be easily embedded or linked to on your company's website, Facebook page, or Twitter feed. Quick, one-or two-minute video clips of rehearsals, interviews featuring different cast and company members, tours of your facility, or other behind-the-scenes footage are easy to shoot and upload. Like updating your company's social media sites, don't let these videos linger for a long time. Create a different video each week and let your audience know to look for new ones. Keep them engaged and returning.

3. *Podcasts*. Much more demanding in terms of time, podcasts allow you the benefit of being in-depth while reaching out to your audience. According to the Pew Research Center, "advances in technology—in particular, the rapid growth in use of smartphones and mobile devices in addition to the increased ease of in-car listening—have contributed to the uptick of interest in podcasts."[5] The same Pew Research Center article notes that the percentage of Americans who listened to

93

podcasts almost doubled between 2008 and 2015 (leaping from 9 percent to 17 percent). Should you choose to create a podcast for your company, look at producing in-depth interviews with company members and production staff. If possible, include playwrights, composers, and musicians too. Cast as wide a net as you can when creating your podcasts, in order to reach as many people as possible.

Whichever method (or methods) you use in promotions and marketing, remember that your goal is to engage with as many potential audience members as possible. You want to excite your current ticket holders, as well as entice future ticket holders with each of your posts, videos, and podcasts.

As mentioned previously in the chapter (and elsewhere in the book), a lot of this information may be considered "non-traditional" for a directing text. In truth, much of this, in many companies, would never be handled by the director. But as we've said, many of you will begin your careers putting shows together on your own and that will require you to wear many hats. Additionally, as you progress in your career, you will find that having a little knowledge in these areas will make it much easier for you to communicate when you are sitting in meetings and discussing a production. Adding to your own base of knowledge and experience will greatly enhance your future endeavors as a director!

Exercises and Suggested Reading

Exercises

1. Use Google Drive, Dropbox, or some other document-sharing service to create a folder for a show (you can use the same one you used for the exercises in Chapter 5). Create a master folder, along with sub-folders that you think you might need. Share the folder with your instructor so you can get used to the collaborative process.
2. Divide into groups or four and create your own theatre company. Give your company a name and choose a four-show season. Use a DIY website-building service and create a virtual callboard for your company. Make sure to delineate sections of your callboard and post information that would be relevant to your company members for each show.

3. Choose one of the shows you used in Exercise 2 and create a social media marketing campaign for it. Use at least two different social media platforms and create content that could be posted. Make use of a content posting calendar, as well.

Notes

1. "Mobile Technology Fact Sheet," accessed August 17, 2015, www.pewinternet.org/fact-sheets/mobile-technology-fact-sheet/.
2. "U.S. Smartphone Use in 2015," April 1, 2015, www.pewinternet.org/2015/04/01/us-smartphone-use-in-2015/.
3. "How Long Do Users Stay on Web Pages," September 12, 2011, www.nngroup.com/articles/how-long-do-users-stay-on-web-pages/.
4. "5 Reasons Why a Social Media Content Calendar is Important for Your Business," accessed August 17, 2015, http://blog.hootsuite.com/how-to-create-a-social-media-content-calendar/.
5. "Podcasting: Fact Sheet," April 29, 2015, www.journalism.org/2015/04/29/podcasting-fact-sheet/.

Suggested Reading 95

Bernstein, Joanne Scheff. *Arts Marketing Insights: The Dynamics of Building and Retaining Performing Arts Audiences* (San Francisco, CA: Jossey-Bass, 2006).

Handley, Ann. *Content Rules: How to Create Killer Blogs, Podcasts, Videos, Ebooks, Webinars (and More) That Engage Customers and Ignite Your Business* (Hoboken, NJ: Wiley Publishing, 2012).

Hyatt, Michael. *Platform: Get Noticed in a Noisy World* (Nashville, TN: Thomas Nelson, 2012).

Kern, Jonathan. *Sound Reporting: The NPR Guide to Audio Journalism and Production* (Chicago, IL: University of Chicago Press, 2008).

O'Reilly, Darragh and Kerrigan, Finola (eds). *Marketing the Arts: A Fresh Approach* (New York: Routledge, 2010).

VanOrden, Jason. *Promoting Your Podcast: The Ultimate Guide to Building an Audience of Raving Fans* (Blue Bell, PA: Larstan Publishing, 2006).

PLANNING AND ORGANIZATION

CHAPTER 7

The Rehearsal Calendar

All of your work throughout this process has led you to this point: the rehearsals! This is the part of production that almost all directors love the most. The opportunity to be in the studio, working with other artists to create and craft the show is what draws and drives directors. In her book about JoAnne Akalaitis, the Mabou Mines founder and former New York Shakespeare Festival Artistic Director, Deborah Saivetz notes that "Akalaitis describes a rehearsal process as a journey that in and of itself is far more important than its destination."[1] The importance of that journey cannot be overstated, as it will ultimately determine the level of success for your production. Before you can get to the rehearsals, though, you have to plan out your rehearsal calendar, which is something of an artform in itself.

Many directors, when scheduling rehearsals, use a simple formula of one hour of rehearsal for every minute of the play. For this reason, six weeks is a relatively standard length for rehearsals in most educational and community theatres, assuming rehearsals average around three hours per night. Of course, there is no definitive formula, as different directors prefer to rehearse for different durations. Directors like Jerzy Grotowski and Peter Brook are famous for leaving rehearsal periods open-ended, focusing (as Akalaitis said) much more on the journey than the destination. Obviously, certain types of shows require more rehearsal time than others: musicals, farce, shows with a lot of stage combat (as an aside, a variation on the one-hour-to-one-minute formula for stage combat is ten hours of rehearsal for each minute of a fight). With experience, you will discover how quickly (or not) you work as a director on different types of play.

Ultimately, you'll come to develop your own formula of how many rehearsals you need to accomplish what you want for your production.

Of course, in professional theatre, you have your company available for rehearsals all day, and not just three hours in the evening. If working with Equity actors, you will have them for most of the day, but you do need to be aware of the Equity rules surrounding rehearsals. Even though adherence to the AEA regulations will fall on others (the Equity deputy, PSM, producer, etc.), as the director you still need to be aware of the rules in a general sense so that you can schedule your actors accordingly. For the majority of a rehearsal period, you can call Equity actors for seven out of eight-and-a-half hours. If you're rehearsing in 55–75-minute blocks, you have to schedule five-minute breaks. Rehearsal blocks of 80 minutes require a ten-minute break. Additionally, Equity actors cannot be called for a rehearsal within 12 hours of the previous rehearsal finishing. As you move into technical rehearsals, you have the opportunity to rehearse ten hours out of 12. All of this information, and more, can be found in the Equity Production Rulebook.[2] All these rules are simple to follow (and require basically no work on your part) if you are directing at a League of Resident Theatres (LORT) company or with a full Equity cast. If, however, you are directing for a company operating under a guest artist contract, you should keep the rules in mind when scheduling, as there will be certain times that one (or two, or however many guest artists you have) of your performers will not be available to you.

On the website accompanying this book, you'll find a "rehearsal calendar planning sheet." This is a simple but effective tool that will allow you to schedule each of your rehearsals, paying particular attention to what you will be rehearsing each day. The biggest thing to remember, when beginning to plan out your rehearsal calendar is not to get *too* specific. That may seem counterintuitive, but the specificity will come as you do your daily rehearsal schedules (which will be addressed in Chapter 8). The calendar is a general guide, to make sure that you are allotting yourself enough time to accomplish all that is needed in the process. The rehearsal calendar's level of detail will depend on the type of show that you are doing. We'll look at some specific examples later, but first let's discuss the actual preparation of the calendar. There are some directors who turn over calendar and scheduling completely to the PSM, but I do *not* recommend that. Unless the PSM is someone with whom you've spent years developing a rapport and who implicitly understands the way you work, you will want to plan out your own rehearsal calendar, as that is the only way you will have a firm grasp of the entire process. So how do you go about doing that? I'm so glad you asked!

Start at the End

The first rehearsal that I put on every calendar I do is the last one: *final dress*. It's truly the one rehearsal that is not up in the air or subject to change. Directors need to be flexible when creating their calendars and going through the process, because you never know what might come up that demands more attention (hence the comment above about not getting too specific). So unless you are of the Brook/Grotowski "infinite rehearsal" school, you know that final dress has to be the last rehearsal before you open. From there, you can work your way backwards through the calendar, making sure that each period of rehearsal (and part of the show) is given what it needs.

Communicate with your Collaborators

When building your rehearsal calendar, it's important to talk with your production team ahead of time, to see how much rehearsal time they think they are going to need. This includes your designers and TD for technical and dress rehearsals, and any other artists who might be working on specialized areas of the show. If you are working on a musical, you will need to consult your music director, choreographer, and possibly your conductor about their needs. If you are doing a show with a lot of stage combat, you will need to talk with your fight choreographer. Does your show have dialects and are you using a vocal coach? Make sure you've spoken with her as well. One thing to bear in mind is that specialty rehearsals for things like choreography (dance or fight) will often take up more time than "regular" acting rehearsals, so you may need to allow for that.

Build in Buffers

The rehearsal process for directors is, in large part, all about being flexible. The unexpected will always arise and the unaccounted for will always be discovered. Where possible, then, you need to include days in the calendar for which you don't have specific plans—TBA days, as it were. By having these already in your schedule, you'll be able to accommodate your fight choreographer much more easily when he tells you he just needs *"one more day"* to finish up the Battle of Agincourt.

Work in Blocks

Remember the exhaustive script analysis you did for your play? One of the practical applications of that analysis is that you can use it to schedule your rehearsal blocks. Since the calendar is general, you can use the script divisions (acts, scenes, French scenes) to mark out blocks for rehearsals. The result of this is that you are able to put on your calendar: "Work Act I, Scenes 1A–4C" on one day, to be followed by "Work Act I, Scenes 4D–6C" on the next. This is really all you need on your calendar, as it gives your company an idea of what they can prepare for each day, and the knowledge that they will get specifics on the daily schedule.

Account for Conflicts

This is where having an excellent PSM helps, but if you are working alone, it is definitely a step you do not want to miss. Assuming you are directing for a non-professional company (otherwise this step becomes largely irrelevant), you will want to go through the conflicts actors listed on their audition forms. In almost all educational, community, and church theatre companies, your actors will have responsibilities outside of the production that may take them away from rehearsal on certain nights. If you're directing Nora Ephron's *Lucky Guy*, you don't want to schedule a day where you are working on a block of scenes featuring Mike (the lead character) if the actor you have playing the role is off at his nephew's wedding rehearsal dinner that night.

As we've said before, flexibility is going to be your friend, as certain unplanned-for events will always crop up. A few more things to bear in mind when creating your calendar:

1. *Location.* Always include the location of the rehearsal on your calendar. Many theatres do not rehearse in the performance space, instead relying on a studio of some kind. Additionally, you may be working for a company that has multiple spaces available for rehearsal (studios, classrooms, etc.), and you want to make sure everyone can find you!

2. *Time.* While most directors (and companies) like to rehearse at the same time each day, there are certainly occasions when rehearsal time has to be changed. Get in the habit of listing the time for each day.
3. *Changes.* This isn't necessarily something that goes on the calendar (although, it could, if you wanted to put it on there), but make sure your company knows where to go in the event of schedule changes. If you're using electronic postings, you can list those changes there and make sure to push the information to the cast.
4. *Deadlines.* Make sure to put your off-book deadlines on the calendar. Most actors like having that reminder for them, so they have a date to plan for when they have to put down their scripts.

To elaborate on the steps mentioned above, let's look at some examples from various types of shows. First, we'll look at a schedule for a straight play—but one which involves some dialect work that must be scheduled: Noël Coward's *Private Lives*.

Figure 7.1 is an image of a rehearsal calendar for *Private Lives*, using the rehearsal planning sheet found on the website. Note that the bottom of the sheet provides you with options for color coding the type of rehearsal you are planning. The colors are arbitrary, so feel free to change them to suit your own aesthetics; the key is to provide a quick reference for actors as they look at the schedule. On this calendar, you see that the director intends to spend a few days on table work and blocking the show (the black days), but the majority of the rehearsal time is taken up with working and running rehearsals (the dark gray days). Since this is a straight play, there aren't any days used for music or choreography rehearsals, but there are a few days given over to dialect work (the light gray days). Oftentimes, *Private Lives* includes a good bit of stage combat, but the lack of that indication on the calendar tells you that the director is planning on addressing any combat needs within working and running rehearsals. You see that the director has clearly indicated time and location for each rehearsal, as well as giving the actors an idea of what will be covered. For a straight play of this complexity 25 rehearsals may be a bit rushed, but you have to assume that the director has a good grasp on how quickly it will be possible to work with the given cast.

Figure 7.2 shows a portion of a rehearsal calendar for a production of *Guys and Dolls*. You see here that the color coding is vital, as

Show: *Private Lives* – Noel Coward

Rehearsal Planning Sheet
Calendar Format

Company: XYZ Theatre Company

Sunday	Monday	Tuesday	Wednesday	Thursday	Friday	Saturday
1　7:30 PM Rehearsal Studio **Read-Thru**	2　7:30 PM Rehearsal Studio **Character Discussion**	3　7:30 PM Rehearsal Studio **Block Act I**	4　7:30 PM Rehearsal Studio **Block Act II**	5　7:30 PM Rehearsal Studio **Block Act III**	6　7:30 PM Rehearsal Studio Stumble-Thru	7　Time ____ Location ____ OFF
8　Time ____ Location ____ OFF	9　7:30 PM Rehearsal Studio *Dialect Work*	10　7:30 PM Rehearsal Studio *Dialect Work*	11　7:30 PM Rehearsal Studio Work Act I Scenes	12　7:30 PM Rehearsal Studio Work Act II Scenes	13　7:30 PM Rehearsal Studio Work Act III Scenes	14　Time ____ Location ____ OFF
15　Time ____ Location ____ OFF	16　7:30 PM Rehearsal Studio Run Act I OFF BOOK!	17　7:30 PM Rehearsal Studio Run Act II OFF BOOK!	18　7:30 PM Rehearsal Studio Run Act III OFF BOOK!	19　7:30 PM Rehearsal Studio *Dialect Touch-Up*	20　7:30 PM Rehearsal Studio *TBA*	21　Time ____ Location ____ OFF
22　1:00 PM XYZ Theatre Load-In to Theatre	23　7:30 PM XYZ Theatre Run-Thru	24　7:30 PM XYZ Theatre Work Scenes – TBA	25　7:30 PM XYZ Theatre Run-Thru	26　7:30 PM XYZ Theatre Work Scenes – TBA	27　7:30 PM XYZ Theatre Run-Thru	28　10:00 PM XYZ Theatre First Tech Rehearsal
29　2:00 PM XYZ Theatre Second Tech Rehearsal	30　7:30 PM XYZ Theatre First Dress Rehearsal	31　7:30 PM XYZ Theatre Final Dress Rehearsal	1　7:30 PM XYZ Theatre **OPENING NIGHT!!**	Date ____ Location ____ Time ____	Date ____ Location ____ Time ____	Date ____ Location ____ Time ____

Black = Table Work/Blocking　　Dark grey = Working/Running　　Light grey = Techs/Dress　　**Black Italic = Music**　　*Dark grey italic = Choreography*　　*Light grey italic = Other*

Director: John Q. Director

Month: March

Figure 7.1 Private Lives rehearsal calendar.

the director is juggling a wide variety of rehearsal types (music, choreography, working, etc.). Notice, too, how important it is to include time and location, as Sunday rehearsals are typically at a different time than weekday rehearsals. Additionally, rehearsals are being held in four different locations, information that is crucial to the actors. As this is (presumably) the second page of the rehearsal calendar, you can assume that the director handled blocking, Act I choreography, and perhaps some working rehearsals prior to what we see here. Again we have an off-book deadline, and the director has built in a TBA rehearsal (on this page) in case one area needs more time. Just as with your working rehearsals, you will want to be broad here, with your descriptions of what will be rehearsed in music and choreography rehearsals, so that your music director and choreographer can set their own schedules on the daily breakdown.

Once again, you see a partial calendar in Figure 7.3—this time for a production of *Macbeth*. We will talk about table-work rehearsals in detail in Chapter 9, but note that oftentimes rehearsals for Shakespeare or other complex shows require extra table-work rehearsals. Also, since we're dealing with Shakespeare in this image, notice how the director has specifically indicated "Shakespeare's Act I" (etc.) in her calendar. This isn't a linguistic oddity, but a necessity. Since Shakespeare doesn't indicate intermissions in his scripts, most directors wind up dividing the script in a way that makes sense for their production. Hence, it's not uncommon to refer to "Shakespeare's Act I" (Act I as it is indicated in the script) and "Our Act I" (which might go from Act I, scene i to Act III, scene v as written in the script). Because the purpose of the rehearsal calendar is to give the actors an idea of how they can prepare, you want to make sure that you're careful in how you refer to sections so that you don't confuse the actors. You also see the first two of what will certainly be multiple stage-combat rehearsals indicated. As with music and choreography in a musical, make sure to allow your fight director the opportunity to schedule specific rehearsals.

As we've said, different types of shows require different rehearsal planning … even different rehearsal schedules. Some directors like to break down rehearsals in list form, as opposed to using a calendar. Figure 7.4 shows you an example from a children's theatre production of *Sleeping Beauty*. Because a large number of children were involved in the show, the cast was broken down into groups, and assistant directors charged with leading each group. Groups were assigned colors for ease of reference and it was easy for the actors (and parents) to see who would be rehearsing where and when.

105

Show: *Guys and Dolls*

Rehearsal Planning Sheet
Calendar Format

Company: XYZ Theatre Company

Sunday	Monday	Tuesday	Wednesday	Thursday	Friday	Saturday
1 2:30 PM Dance Studio *Act II Choreography*	2 6:00 PM Dance Studio *Act II Choreography*	3 6:00 PM Dance Studio *Act II Choreography*	4 6:00 PM Dance Studio *Choreography Brush-Up*	5 6:00 PM Choir Room ***Act I Music Review***	6 6:00 PM Choir Room ***Act II Music Review***	7 Location ____ Time ____ OFF
8 2:30 PM Choir Room ***Solo Work***	9 6:00 PM Rehearsal Hall Run Act I	10 6:00 PM Rehearsal Studio Run Act II	11 6:00 PM Rehearsal Studio Run Act I OFF BOOK	12 6:00 PM Rehearsal Studio Run Act I	13 6:00 PM Rehearsal Studio Run Act II OFF BOOK	14 Location ____ Time ____ OFF
15 2:30 PM TBA TBA	16 6:00 PM STAGE Run-Thru	17 6:00 PM STAGE Run-Thru	18 6:00 PM STAGE *Choreography Brush-Up*	19 6:00 PM STAGE ***Music Brush-Up***	20 6:00 PM STAGE Run-Thru	21 STAGE TECH ACT I TBA
22 TBA STAGE TECH ACT II	23 6:00 PM STAGE Tech Rehearsal	24 6:00 PM STAGE Tech/Dress	25 7:30 PM STAGE First Dress	26 7:30 PM STAGE Final Dress	27 7:30 PM STAGE OPENING NIGHT!	28 Date ____ Location ____ Time ____
29 Time ____ Location ____	30 Time ____ Location ____	Date ____ Location ____ Time ____	Date ____ Location ____ Time ____	Date ____ Location ____ Time ____	Date ____ Location ____ Time ____	Date ____ Location ____ Time ____

Black = Table Work/Blocking   Dark grey = Working/Running   Light grey = Techs/Dress   ***Black Italic = Music***   Dark grey italic = Choreography   *Light grey Italic = Other*

Director: Jane Q. Director

Month: June

Figure 7.2 Guys and Dolls rehearsal calendar (partial).

Show: *Macbeth*

Rehearsal Planning Sheet
Calendar Format

Company: XYZ Theatre Company

Sunday	Monday	Tuesday	Wednesday	Thursday	Friday	Saturday
1 Time ___ Location ___	2 Time ___ Location ___	3 Time ___ Location ___	4 Time ___ Location ___	5 Time ___ Location ___	6 Time ___ Location ___	7 Time ___ Location ___
8 Time ___ Location ___	9 Time ___ Location ___	10 Time ___ Location ___	11 Time ___ Location ___	12 7:00 PM Rehearsal Hall AUDITIONS	13 7:00 PM Rehearsal Hall AUDITIONS	14 3:00 PM Rehearsal Hall Call Backs
15 Time ___ Location ___	16 7:00 PM Classroom 142 **Read-Thru**	17 7:00 PM Classroom 142 **Read-Thru**	18 7:00 PM Classroom 142 **Table Work – History**	19 7:00 PM Classroom 142 **Table Work – Language**	20 7:00 PM Rehearsal Hall *Weapons Orientation*	21 Time ___ Location ___
22 Time ___ Location ___	23 7:00 PM Rehearsal Hall **Block Shakespeare's Act I**	24 7:00 PM Rehearsal Hall **Block Shakespeare's Act II**	25 7:00 PM Rehearsal Hall **Block Shakespeare's Act III**	26 7:00 PM Rehearsal Hall **Block Shakespeare's Act IV**	27 7:00 PM Rehearsal Hall **Block Shakespeare's Act V**	28 Time ___ Location ___
29	30 7:00 PM Rehearsal Hall *Fight Choreography*	Date ___ Time ___ Location ___	Date ___ Time ___ Location ___	Date ___ Time ___ Location ___	Date ___ Time ___ Location ___	Date ___ Time ___ Location ___

Black = Table Work/Blocking   Dark grey = Working/Running   Light grey = Techs/Dress   ***Black Italic = Music***   *Dark grey italic = Choreography*   *Light grey italic = Other*

Director: Jane Q. Director

Month: April

Figure 7.3 Macbeth rehearsal calendar (partial).

DAY	TIME	ACTING GROUP	DIR/AD	LOCATION	TO WORK
Mon. 1/4	6:00 PM	Green Group	Alexis	Stone	Review Act I Blocking
		Yellow Group	Austin	Howard Lobby	Review Act I Blocking
		Blue Group	Millie	Howard	Review Act I Blocking
		Red Group	Jess	Acting Studio	Review Act I Blocking
	7:30 PM	Brown Group	Paul	Howard	Stumble-Thru Show
Tues. 1/5	6:00 PM	Green Group	Alexis	Stone	Review Act II Blocking
		Yellow Group	Austin	Howard Lobby	Review Act II Blocking
		Blue Group	Millie	Howard	Review Act II Blocking
		Red Group	Jess	Acting Studio	Review Act II Blocking
	7:30 PM	Brown Group	Paul	Howard	Selected Scene Work
Wed. 1/6	6:00 PM	ALL	ALL	Howard	Stumble-Thru
Thur. 1/7	6:00 PM	Green Group	Alexis	Stone	Act I Work
		Yellow Group	Austin	Howard Lobby	Act I Work
		Blue Group	Millie	Howard	Act I Work
		Red Group	Jess	Acting Studio	Act I Work
	7:30 PM	Brown Group	Paul	Howard	Act I Work
Fri. 1/8	5:30 PM	Green Group	Alexis	Stone	Act II Work
		Yellow Group	Austin	Howard Lobby	Act II Work
		Blue Group	Millie	Howard	Act II Work
		Red Group	Jess	Acting Studio	Act II Work
	7:00 PM	Brown Group	Paul	Howard	Act II Work

Figure 7.4 Sleeping Beauty rehearsal calendar (partial).

As you can see, while not particularly specific with what is being rehearsed (that comes later), the schedule lets everyone know when they need to be present and where they will be working.

Before we leave the rehearsal calendar, a reminder of the importance of flexibility as you plot out your overall rehearsal structure. Whether it's an illness or an injury to a company member, a blizzard that keeps people from being able to make it to rehearsal, or unplanned construction that means you can't get into your facility, things will happen that are well beyond your control. Your planning, knowledge, and preparation will allow you to deal with the unexpected gracefully.

Exercises and Suggested Reading

Exercises

1. Read Pearl Cleage's *Blues for an Alabama Sky* and create a rehearsal schedule for a production. Assume that you are directing at your school and follow the appropriate timeframe for rehearsals. Use the rehearsal calendar planning sheet found on the website.

2. Read Cole Porter's *Kiss Me Kate* and create a rehearsal schedule for a production. Assume that you are directing at a community theatre and have seven weeks from auditions to opening night. You will not have actors available for any Saturday or Sunday rehearsals until the weekend before the show opens. Use the rehearsal calendar planning sheet found on the website.

3. Read Ken Ludwig's *The Three Musketeers* and create a rehearsal schedule for a production. Assume that you are working at a small professional theatre company (non-Equity) and have 17 days from first rehearsal to opening night. Even though you are at a non-Equity house, use the information found in the Equity handbook online to adhere to time regulations. Use the rehearsal calendar planning sheet found on the website.

Notes

1. Deborah Saivetz, *An Event in Space: JoAnne Akalaitis in Rehearsal* (Hanover, NH: Smith and Krauss, Inc., 2000), *xv*.

2. "Actor's Equity Association Agreement and Rules Governing Employment Under the Equity/League Production Contract," accessed August 19, 2015, www.actorsequity.org/docs/rulebooks/Production_Rulebook_League_11–15.pdf.

Suggested Reading

Cleage, Pearl. *Blues for an Alabama Sky* (New York: Dramatists Play Service, 1995).

Ephron, Nora. *Lucky Guy* (New York: Dramatists Play Service, 2013).

Grotowski, Jerzy. *Towards a Poor Theatre* (New York: Routledge, 2002 (1968)).

Loesser, Frank (music and lyrics), Burrows, Abe, and Swerling, Jo (book). *Guys and Dolls* (New York: Musical Theatre International, 1950).

Ludwig, Ken. *The Three Musketeers* (New York: Samuel French, 2010).

Porter, Cole (music and lyrics), Spewack, Samuel, and Spewack, Bella (book). *Kiss Me Kate* (New York: Tams-Witmark, 1948).

Saivetz, Deborah. *An Event in Space: JoAnne Akalaitis in Rehearsal* (Hanover, NH: Smith and Kraus, Inc., 2000).

Shakespeare, William. *Macbeth* (*c.*1599–1606, available online).

110

CHAPTER 8

Scheduling Rehearsals

One of the biggest keys to scheduling individual rehearsals is to avoid wasting time—your own and that of your cast, crew, and production staff. It seems like a pretty simple premise, but you would be surprised at how often that admonition is ignored. Well, if you've been in many rehearsals yourself, you might not be surprised at all. A common phrase in theatre that we've all heard (usually around our freshman year after walking into a rehearsal as the minute hand is clicking onto the hour, and delivered by the stage manager in an icy tone) is: "On time is late; early is on time." We demand that our actors be mindful and courteous of the company's time, so it stands to reason that, as directors, we should do the same. Another all-too-common experience that most actors have had at least once is that of sitting in a rehearsal hall for three-plus hours, only to have the director turn and say, "Jeez, I'm sorry I didn't get to you tonight." Does your blood pressure begin to rise while merely reading that? It should. While there are certainly going to be rehearsals where having actors sit for long periods is unavoidable (blocking rehearsals, run-throughs, etc.), the more work you do to keep those to a minimum, the more appreciation you will receive from your cast and the better the company's morale will be.

The secret to making the most efficient use of your time is planning. It began with the script analysis that you did (especially the character-scene-location breakdown), which ensures that you have a firm foundational grasp of your production, and continues with your preparation before each rehearsal. In Chapter 7, we discussed the importance of not getting too specific with your rehearsal calendar;

the individual rehearsal scheduling is where you get to be more specific. Using your calendar as the broad roadmap for rehearsals, you will be able to plot out your specific plan for individual rehearsals. Typically, I like to sit with my PSM at the end of each rehearsal to plan out the next one. While stage management is usually in charge of the rehearsal forms and making sure calls are posted, it's important for you to have an idea of how to do this on your own. Additionally, as we've said regarding other areas of production, most of you will begin by having to wear multiple hats—including serving as your own stage manager! To that end, there is a rehearsal schedule planning sheet available on the website. Let's take some time and go over the elements of the planning sheet and look at how it can be used.

The top portion of the sheet is self-explanatory, but I will re-emphasize the importance of including time and location, just as you did on the calendar. The left-hand column divides your rehearsal into "blocks," which is merely an easy way to identify and refer to individual portions of rehearsal. Using this method allows you a quick way to communicate with both your cast and the production team when talking about the day's rehearsal. The sheet provides spaces for eight rehearsal blocks, though on any given day you may find that you either don't need that many or

Rehearsal Schedule Planning Sheet

Show Title: _____   Rehearsal Date: _____

Rehearsal #: _____   Location: _____   Start Time: _____

Block	Start Time	End Time	Type	To Be Rehearsed	Actors Called
A					
B					
C					
D					
E					
F					
G					
H					

Notes: _____

_____

TWB=Table Work/Blocking WR=Working/Running TD=Tech/Dress M=Music C=Choreography O=Other

Figure 8.1 The rehearsal schedule planning sheet.

you need more. Obviously, the form can be adjusted to suit your needs.

The next two columns, "start time" and "end time," will (with the exception of the start of your A-Block) be a bit malleable. You may have your C-Block scheduled to begin at 8:15, but because your A-Block ran five minutes long you might not start it until 8:20. Conversely, you may have your E-Block scheduled for a 9:20 start time, but because you were able to cut in half the time needed for the D-block you now find you can begin at 9:10. The more experience you gain working with a cast, the easier you will find it to predict how long it will take you to accomplish what needs to be done in a given rehearsal block.

The fourth column, labeled "type," utilizes the same color coding as the rehearsal calendar. It also uses the same terminology for the different types of rehearsal: you can see the key at the bottom of the page. While it's always good to use a planning sheet, the farther along you get in the rehearsal process, the more simple it will become. Once you get to run-throughs, technical rehearsals, and dress rehearsals, you will often use only one block, indicating that the run will begin at a given time. In those rehearsals, when every actor is called for the entirety of the rehearsal, the breakdown isn't always necessary.

113

The contents of the "to be rehearsed" column will vary, depending on the type of show and the type of rehearsal. For small straight plays, you may decide simply to use act and scene numbers, or even only page numbers, to let your company know what to expect. Larger casts, musicals, combat-heavy shows, or others might require you to identify the material to be rehearsed in a different fashion. Song titles, such as "Sunrise" if you're directing *In The Heights*, or descriptions, such as "final knife fight" if you're directing *The Illusion*, may be appropriate to list instead of page, act, or scene numbers. The most important factor is that you are clear with what will be rehearsed in that block. Actors work best when they are able to prepare for rehearsals (a somewhat obvious statement, I know), which means that knowing *what* they need to prepare is key.

The final column, "actors called," is probably more necessary than you realize. While it might be tempting to assume that an actor seeing "Act II, scene iii" in the "to be rehearsed" column would know to be present if he or she is in that scene, it would be wrong to make that assumption. Actors often (in their own minds and/or research notebooks) often break down and refer to a show in a manner different from that found in the script. Because of this, they may think of "Act II, scene iii" as "the scene in the church." Thus, if an actor doesn't see his or her name specifically on the call sheet, it's easy for confusion to ensue.

The final section of the sheet is a kind of catch-all that allows you to make the cast aware of anything special for the next day's rehearsal. Is the B-Block of rehearsal going to take place in the choir room? Are they supposed to be off-book? Is there a newspaper photographer coming? Are they working in character shoes? Just about anything can go in the "Notes" section. Most actors are, to a certain extent, creatures of habit. They are used to coming into rehearsal at a certain time, and they have their routine down. Anything that deviates from the routine has the potential to affect an actor's rehearsal negatively, which is why it's important to prepare them for anything out of the ordinary.

To get an idea of what a completed sheet looks like, look at Figure 8.2.

A few things to notice:

- The "location" line indicates both locations where rehearsals will be held.
- The "type" column is color coded to match the key on the bottom.

Rehearsal Schedule Planning Sheet

Show Title: **The Producers**   Rehearsal Date: **06/16**

Rehearsal #: **12**   Location: **Rehearsal Hall, Dance Studio**   Start Time: **6:30 PM**

Block	Start Time	End Time	Type	To Be Rehearsed	Actors Called
A	6:30 pm	7:15 pm	WR	I, i Placement and spacing on staging of "Opening Night" and "King of Old Broadway"	ALL
B	7:15 pm	7:40 pm	WR	I, ix Clean up business going into and getting out of the song.	ALL
C	7:50 pm	8:25 pm	M	"That Face"	Mickey S. and Phyllis M.
D	7:50 pm	8:25 pm	C	Clean "Along Came Bialy" choreography	Jane W, Alexis P, Tish S, Alexis R, Clara O, Donna N, Rose T, Martha J, Amy P, Ann M, Jack H.
E	8:25 pm	9:00 pm	C	Work-thru "I Wanna Be A Producer"	Jane W, Alexis P, Tish S, Alexis R, Clara O, Donna N, Rose T, Martha J, Amy P, Ann M, Mickey S.
F	8:25 pm	9:00 pm	M	"Betrayed"	Jack H.
G	9:10 pm	9:30 pm	WR	I, ii Work on crosses and cleaning for staging of "We Can Do It."	Jack H. and Mickey S.
H					

Notes: D-Block will be in Dance Studio at the same time as C-Block is in the Rehearsal Hall.

E-Block will be in Dance Studio at the same time as F-Block is in the Rehearsal Hall.

TWB=Table Work/Blocking   WR=Working/Running   TD=Tech/Dress   M=Music   C=Choreography   O=Other

Figure 8.2 Rehearsal planning sheet for *The Producers*.

- There is a ten-minute gap between the end time of the B-Block and the beginning of C-block. Additionally, there is a ten-minute gap between the end of F-Block and the beginning of G-Block. These are intentional, and represent when breaks will be taken.

- Aside from the two music blocks (C and F), there is a good bit of information found in the "to be rehearsed" column. This lets the actors know exactly what they can expect when they get to those blocks of rehearsal. The aforementioned music blocks just have the titles of the songs to be worked.

- The "notes" section alleviates any confusion at the fact that there are two blocks rehearsing at the same time.

- If you scan down the "actors called" column, you will notice that the number of actors called for each block dwindles as the night wears on, from everyone in the cast at the beginning of the rehearsal to only the actors playing Max and Leo at the end. Particularly in working rehearsals, I find it best to start with scenes (or numbers) that require the most cast members first, and pare down as the rehearsal progresses. This allows you to release actors as you go along, rather than calling large numbers of actors in late in the rehearsal. Particularly in an educational or community theatre setting, it's a tough thing for an actor to be called at 9:00 at night.

Working in this fashion (grouping scenes to be worked by how many actors are called) is the way you are able to guarantee that you are using everyone's time as efficiently as possible. This requires, usually, that you work scenes out of sequential order. Most actors are used to working in this manner, and don't have a problem with it; usually it is something that first-time directors have to get used to, as it seems a bit counterintuitive. However, the more solid your script analysis is, the more comfortable you will be jumping around in rehearsals. Obviously, the farther along in the process you get—when you are running the show every night—the less opportune this approach becomes. You will find, though, that having been conscientious of taking up actors' time early in the process will make them much more amenable when technical rehearsals roll around, requiring everyone to adhere to the old military axiom of "hurry up and wait."

As we've seen, being specific and thoughtful when scheduling the rehearsals allows your actors to be prepared for each day, but how do you get yourself prepared? How do you, as a director, make

115

Rehearsal Goals and Evaluation Sheet

Director Name: _____

Show Title: _____

Rehearsal Date: _____   Rehearsal #: _____

GOAL(S)	HOW TO ACCOMPLISH

SUCCESS?	EVALUATION

ACTION PLAN

Figure 8.3 The rehearsal goals and evaluation sheet.

certain that you enter each rehearsal with a clear vision and plan of what you need to accomplish? Just like you did for your actors, you need to give yourself a detailed and specific breakdown for each rehearsal. The best tool for doing this is journaling, which should be done for *each* rehearsal. On the website accompanying this book, you will find the "rehearsal goals and evaluation sheet" that serves as the template for your directing journal.

Notice that, once again, you need to be specific about the date and number of the rehearsal. This is, ultimately, so you can organize everything and easily reference it in the future. The top two boxes on the sheet, "goal(s)" and "how to accomplish," should be filled out *prior* to each rehearsal. The bottom three boxes, "success," "evaluation," and "action plan" are to be filled out *after* each rehearsal.

Goal(s) (complete prior to rehearsal)

As a director, you should approach every rehearsal with a goal (often more than one) in mind of what you need to accomplish that day. Rehearsal goals can be:

- basic ("Finish blocking Act II");
- detailed ("Speed up the scene change between I, iii and I, iv. We have to get it down to less than nine seconds");
- educational ("Improve Mark and Sam's spontaneity in II, ii");
- esoteric ("Work on the chemistry between Sara and Adam on the kiss");
- utilitarian ("Work on the pacing in Act III").

This is by no means an exhaustive list. The goals that you set for yourself for each rehearsal will be specific to you and your production. The most important thing is that you set your goals, so that you can go into each rehearsal with a plan.

How to Accomplish (complete prior to rehearsal)

Simply having a goal, though, is not enough. You have to have an idea of how you are going to address the challenge implied in the goal. This is what allows you to rehearse efficiently and effectively, and allows your cast to feel comfort in knowing that the show is moving forward in good hands. Your list of how to accomplish your goals should (obviously) correspond to the individual goals you set. Much like setting goals, this list has a wide range of possibilities. Look at the examples, which correspond to the examples in the previous section:

- basic (block Act II);
- detailed (rehearse the change with crew only, prior to rehearsal; start top of rehearsal by adding in cast; adjust traffic patterns if needed);
- educational (use a couple of improvisation games, such as "archeology" and "freeze frame," to get them thinking creatively on their feet);
- esoteric (try working through the scene with actors visibly playing their psychological gestures to see if that helps them connect);
- utilitarian (do a quick speed-through of the act after the break).

Like the first list, this is definitely not exhaustive—nor is it the only way one could accomplish each of the items on the list. But each of these represents a definite *plan* to reach the goal. Whether or not they work is what you deal with in the next sections, after the rehearsal is over.

Success? (complete after rehearsal)
Typically, after a rehearsal is completed, the first thing I like to do is to sit with my PSM and go over the plan for the next rehearsal. Immediately after that, though, while everything is still fresh in my mind, I do a quick "post-mortem" on the rehearsal just completed. This section is merely a place to write "Yes" or "No," with the occasional "Kind of" thrown in for goals that were partially reached.

Evaluation (complete after rehearsal)
Here is where your intelligence, analytical skills, and *honesty* come into play. This section is the "why?" or "why not?" companion to the previous section. If you reached your goal, ask yourself why it seemed to work so well. Putting the answer down in writing will allow you to identify practices that work, so you can repeat and build on them in the future. The goals that are not reached, however, is where your honesty (and other intellectual faculties) comes into play. When something doesn't go well, or doesn't work at all, there is a *big* temptation to think, "Well, they just didn't get it." *Do not give in to that temptation.* Be honest with yourself and take responsibility (we'll talk about this much more in Chapter 10); look for how you could have approached the challenge better. As you discover the answer to this, it will lead you to the next, final section.

Action Plan (complete after rehearsal)
For the things that *didn't* work in rehearsal, what are you going to do to improve next time? If you didn't achieve the desired goal for a rehearsal, that means there is a challenge that still needs addressing. As the old saying goes, "Insanity is doing the same thing over and over again, and expecting different results." So, since you want a different result, what will you do differently when you are next confronted with the same issue? This doesn't just have to deal with goals that weren't reached: you can always improve—even on your successes.

To get a better feel for how the goals and evaluation sheet can be used, let's look at an example. Figure 8.4 shows a sample page from a directing journal for a production of Suzan-Lori Parks' *Topdog/Underdog*.

You see that the director has three primary goals for the rehearsal. Working the card business and fixing a problem with an entrance are

118

Rehearsal Goals and Evaluation Sheet

Director Name: ▮▮▮▮▮▮▮▮

Show Title: _Topdog/Underdog_

Rehearsal Date: 9/26   Rehearsal #: ___8___

GOAL(S)	HOW TO ACCOMPLISH
1. Work Booth's 3-card shuffle at top 2. Fix Link's entrance and Booth pulling the gun 3. Address issue of status once Link enters	1. Show the YouTube videos Marsha bookmarked. Pay attention to the patter. 2. Adjust Booth's placement right before the entrance. 3. Discuss ideas with actors

SUCCESS?	EVALUATION
1. Partial 2. Yes 3. No	1. He's getting better at it, but just watching the videos won't be enough. It will take a lot of rehearsing. 2. Having Booth DR instead of DL cleans up the sight lines. 3. I think they _kind of_ understood what I was trying to get across, but I didn't communicate it well enough. I didn't connect it with the title theme enough.

ACTION PLAN
1. I've set up times outside of rehearsal to work with him on his shuffling. I have to make sure that he knows he has to understand how to be good before he can play it poorly onstage. 2. Keep checking in on sight lines in ALL of the scenes. 3. I have a couple of status exercises that we can do to start off rehearsal. Also, I have the article from the library that talks about how the title of the play connects with the show. I will make sure to have copies for both actors.

119

Figure 8.4 A goals/evaluation sheet from _Topdog/Underdog_.

both pretty technical challenges. The third goal, an issue of status between the characters, is much more "artsy." The director has been quite specific in the "how to accomplish" section, identifying the methods for approaching each of the goals. Though the sheet contains a lot of detail, it only lists the manner in which the director will go about each goal, rather than including detailed steps. When we advocate for specificity, there is a limit. If you spend _too_ long writing, then you'll never actually get to putting your ideas into practice.

In the second part of the form, the director indicates the success (or, in one case, lack of success) in reaching these goals. The evaluation of the first goal—which was partially successful—includes perfectly logical reasoning as to why it wasn't completely successful. You can't expect someone to master a three-card monte shuffle after one viewing of a video. The second goal (involving cleaning blocking and sightlines), is adjudged successful in a clinical style. The final goal (the status issue) was not reached. Notice, in the evaluation of the lack of success, the director takes responsibility for falling short of the goal. The director understands that it is her job to make her point to the actors, and part of that job is seeking alternative means of communicating ideas when the first method doesn't work.

The final portion of the sheet is (rightly) more detailed than the previous ones. This is where our director examines what she can do to improve for the next rehearsal and, by extension, help the cast improve. As we said above, her evaluation of the first goal's partial success was logical in recognizing that she is asking the actor to master a specific skill. She goes on to show her understanding further, by indicating how she can continue to be of help to the actor as he rehearses the skill needed. For the final, troublesome, goal, the director began with a perfectly logical plan of having a discussion with the actors. As she noticed that that was not successful, she has developed an action plan that will let her address the show's need in another manner. Some actors respond to extended and theoretical discussions, and some do not. Our director has recognized this and is shifting her approach in an effort to find the best way to reach the actors and help them give the performance the show needs.

Helping the actors give their best performance is, of course, one of the director's primary jobs. You will never be successful until you develop solid habits that allow you to plan for *how* you are going to try to help them at each rehearsal. Used on a daily basis, the goals and evaluation sheet will eventually make up a completed directing journal. Coupled with your script analysis and director's prompt book, you will then have a complete reference source for each show you direct. While photographic and video archives are great for jogging the memory, nothing takes the place of all of this material when you want to reference a show later. Additionally, as intellectual copyright laws protecting the work of directors are scarce to non-existent, this provides a record of your work, should that ever be a question which needs to be addressed.

While the paperwork aspect of rehearsal planning (and evaluating) can sometimes be tedious, it will absolutely pay off once you actually get into rehearsals. All of the preparation by a director is aimed at ensuring that he or she is armed with as much knowledge as possible once the rehearsal process begins.

Exercises and Suggested Reading

Exercises

1. Choose one of the plays from the exercises in Chapter 7. Using the rehearsal schedule planning sheet found on the website, schedule three mock rehearsals. One should deal primarily with table work, one should be a working/running rehearsal, and one a technical rehearsal.
2. Choose a play from the Chapter 7 exercises (different than the one you used in Exercise 1), and select a scene from the show that you wish to direct in class. Use the rehearsal goals and evaluation sheet found on the website to plan and evaluate your rehearsal.

Suggested Reading

Brooks, Mel. *The Producers* (New York: Musical Theatre International, 2001).

Kushner, Tony. *The Illusion* (translated and adapted from Pierre Corneille) (New York: Broadway Play Publishing, 2003 (1988)).

Larson, Jennifer. *Understanding Suzan-Lori Parks* (Columbia, SC: University of South Carolina Press, 2012).

Miranda, Lin-Manuel. *In the Heights* (New York: Rodgers and Hammerstein Library, 2008 (1999)).

Parks, Suzan-Lori. *Topdog/Underdog* (New York: Theatre Communications Group, 2001).

Spolin, Viola. *Improvisation for the Theatre* (Chicago, IL: Northwestern University 1999 (1963)).

Spolin, Viola. *Theatre Games for Rehearsal: A Director's Handbook* (Chicago, IL: Northwestern University Press, 1985).

PART IV

THE DIRECTOR IN REHEARSAL

CHAPTER 9

Table Work and Blocking

I was once in a production of Thornton Wilder's classic, *Our Town*. For a solid week, we sat around a table at each rehearsal and had detailed discussions about character biographies, desires, motivations, and life-choices. By the time we got on our feet and actually began the process of rehearsing the show, almost the entire cast were so tied up in trying to incorporate everything that had been discussed, we were unable to play, experiment, grow, and develop truly three-dimensional characters onstage. I was also once in a production of *Richard II* where we began blocking the show during the second rehearsal ... and completed the blocking three nights before opening. The resulting performances were sloppy and confused, as actors were unsure which version of the blocking to follow and where to go onstage.

The point, then, of those two anecdotes would be, I suppose, "moderation in all things." The American director and Peter Brook collaborator Charles Marowitz has said that "sometimes the most acute direction consists of those things the director has the good sense *not* to discuss."[1] Table work and blocking are obviously necessary to the rehearsal process in some degree or form, but, as we've said before, you have to make sure that you're working efficiently. "More" is not always equivalent to "better." The rehearsal period is finite, and opening night is a hard deadline. That means that you have a set amount of rehearsal time to get all of the different periods of rehearsal in (table work/blocking, working/running, techs/dresses—not to mention any specialty rehearsals that might be required). So how do you accomplish all of this? I'm glad you asked.

Table Work

Let's begin by examining what is included in the term "table work," and how you can utilize it most efficiently. I will preface this section by reiterating that this is certainly not the *only* way to approach the rehearsal process, but it is a foundational approach that will serve you well as you gain more and more experience and discover the manner of working that is best for you. With that in mind, here are some of the activities that fall under the "table work" umbrella.

Read-Throughs

The most common type of table work rehearsal, we're all familiar with read-throughs, but have you ever stopped to think about the purpose behind them? Certainly for actors, the read-through often provides the first contact with the full script. For directors, though, the read-through provides an opportunity to learn how good your casting choices were and to begin to get a feel for the what the shape of the show will be. One of the big things to guard against in a read-through is letting actors make character and performance decisions. It's common for an actor to begin making choices immediately, but they haven't done any of their own research and study of the character yet. Because of that, if allowed to make decisive choices, they are often shallow and obvious. A key phrase, which I repeat to actors at every read-through, is: "You've got the gig." I go on to let them know that the read-through is not the time to "act," but simply to read, question, and make notes for later. Douglas Turner Ward, the founder and artistic director of the Negro Ensemble Company, goes further, saying, "Look, you're hired. That already tells you I like you, I want you, you're full of dazzle. You don't have to prove anything more to me, so let's see how we can realize this particular play."[2] In order to begin "realizing" the play, there are three things I like to discover at the read-through. First, what does the show sound like—what is its musicality and rhythm? Second, which actors are bringing interesting ideas that I haven't considered to the table? Finally, is the cast connecting in the way that I expected? You aren't going to get hard and fast answers to these (or any other) questions, but you will begin to get an idea of how the show is going to form.

In addition to reading the script, the first read-through is the best time to have the production team make design presentations and provide the cast with any dramaturgical information they may need to begin their journey with the play. In his afterword to *Camino Real*,

Tennessee Williams famously wrote that the "printed script of a play is hardly more than an architect's blueprint of a house not yet built."[3] The read-through is going to provide the foundation upon which your house will be built.

Dramaturgy

While you may get into some initial dramaturgical information in a read-through, many times there is a lot more detail to bring to the table for your actors. Rehearsals that focus on dramaturgical information are great assets to a company in certain situations. The amount (and type) of dramaturgical information you want to provide a cast truly depends on the type of show you're doing. It may be providing cultural information on members of the early-twentieth-century Jewish upper classes in Atlanta for *The Last Night of Ballyhoo*, or historical background for the homeless in pre-Revolutionary Russia for *The Lower Depths*, or a primer on "the Language of the Fan" for *The Way of the World*.

Dramaturgical information is a great tool to share with your cast, but you don't want to overload them with too much material. In your own research and script analysis, your dramaturgy was integral in forming your ideas for the production. Likewise, it was instrumental in sharing ideas with the design team. With actors, though, there is such a thing as "paralysis by analysis." You need to give them information that is important in helping them make informed and intelligent choices onstage, but you shouldn't bog them down. As a director, it's really easy (and natural) to fall in love with your own research. You've spent so much time on it and it has become so vital to your production, it's natural that you want to share it with everyone, but when you spend too much time going through historical or stylistic information with the cast, you risk becoming *too* cognitive. When that happens, you wind up with actors who are thinking more and acting less ... which is not the recipe for a successful show.

Vocal Work

Whether working on dialects for a production of *Hay Fever* or going over scansion for *King John*, vocal work is some of the most important that you can do at the table. Much of what you will want your actors to work on vocally will be handled in later rehearsals, but verbally intricate shows like these will require some preliminary work while seated. Especially working with younger or less experienced casts, you will want to spend some time introducing them to vocal concepts needed for the production. The one assumption made here is that you will be covering information that will be beneficial to the entire cast. If, however, you only have one or two actors who will have specific vocal demands made on them, then it would be more beneficial to have them work directly with you (or a vocal coach) outside of regular rehearsals. Make certain that you are working in as efficient a manner as possible.

Character Work/Script Analysis

Many directors like to spend time at the table going over script and character analysis with the cast. Developing character biographies and backstories, examining arcs and themes, and exploring relationships are all elements that are discussed at these rehearsals. Working in this manner allows you and your company an opportunity to share ideas about the production and ensure that everyone is on the same page moving forward. I include this section because there are quite a few directors who like working on these things at the table. In Arthur Bartow's collection of interviews, Broadway director Des McAnuff talks about spending between ten and 14 days out of a five-week rehearsal around a table. "What comes out of it," McAnuff says, "is a much deeper group understanding of the piece."[4] Not all directors share that thought, though. Recounting a conversation she had with a Russian director, Anne Bogart refers to the "exquisite pressure" of attention when actors are up on their feet. "No actors actually want to perform their scene sitting around a table."[5] I tend to fall into Bogart's camp, and have found that character and analytical discussions are more beneficial to actors as part of working rehearsals ... when they're up on their feet. The word "acting," after all, is derived from the Latin verb, *agere*, which means "to do." Each of you, however, will figure out which way works best for you, the more often you go through it.

Blocking

Speaking of one of JoAnne Akalaitis' strengths, Deborah Saivetz says that the director "has a striking sense of theatrical composition and is a skilled choreographer of actors' bodies in theatrical space."[6] This is an excellent description of what blocking truly is. Directors use actors to sculpt space and create pictures for the audience. Many would argue that the visual aspect of a performance is the most important. After all, most of us typically go to "see a play" and not to "listen to a play." (As an aside, in Elizabethan theatre, many times it was common for audiences to go to "hear a play," a small point to note how conventions and tastes have changed through the years.) Your blocking is going to emphasize, inform, and elaborate on the story of the script, so it needs to be visually arresting. As we mentioned when talking about casting, there's no "magic bullet" I can give you to make your blocking instantly interesting, but there are things you can do to ensure your blocking is compelling for the audience. In this section, we will discuss some tips for blocking, and examine methods of blocking notation.

Tips for Blocking

1. In Chapter 3, you learned the importance of telling the story. Your blocking is one of the key tools you have to do this. When you block a show, what you are really doing is creating stage pictures. Much like a quality piece of furniture, though, form and function must both be present. In other words, your blocking has to be utilitarian as well as artful. You absolutely have to consider the logistics of where an actor *needs* to be so that everything in the script can be accomplished, but you also must take into account *how* you want actors to accomplish their necessary tasks. Seek to create interesting, visually stimulating pictures as you sculpt the space with your actors.

   Many directors like to think in terms of "snapshot" moments. A snapshot moment is a moment that, like an excellent photograph, sticks in the audience's mind long after they've seen it. These moments often (and rightly) come at climactic points in the show, so that you are underscoring the action and the text with your stage picture. By doing so, you leave the audience with an image that becomes strongly identifiable and associated with your show. Though there's no way to teach a director to have an artistic eye, look for those elements of composition (color, contrast, line, and style) that naturally complement one another in a given moment on stage. Figures 9.1 and 9.2 show some examples of "snapshot moments."

   The final moment of *Grapes of Wrath* is a powerful one, with Rose of Sharon, having lost her baby, nursing a man on the brink of death in Galati's adaptation of the Steinbeck classic. Notice how the isolation of the two forms in an

Figure 9.1 The final scene from Frank Galati's *Grapes of Wrath*. (L–R: Amanda Tatum and Chris Tamez. Photo courtesy of Mark D. Guinn and the Louisiana Tech University Department of Theatre.)

130

Figure 9.2 Macbeth and the three witches from *Macbeth*. (Clockwise from top: Ryan Gentry, Holly Bricker Porch, Amanda Tatum, Payton Wilburn Carnahan. Photo courtesy of Mark D. Guinn and the Louisiana Tech University Department of Theatre.)

almost empty space captures the attention of the viewer, providing an image intended to stay with the audience long after they've left the theatre.

In this scene from *Macbeth*, two elements of the blocking help make this a snapshot moment. The first is the use of levels, with Macbeth seeming to grow, weed-like, out of the witches. Second, notice that each actor is presenting a different look to the audience: Macbeth is facing the audience straight-on, one witch (SL of Macbeth) is in full profile, one (DS of Macbeth) has her back to the audience, and the final witch is in partial profile. The variance in presentation helps this moment of blocking become a memorable one for the audience.

2. I was once in a production of *Romeo and Juliet* that had one of the most beautiful scenic designs I have ever seen. Fully 30 feet in depth, and spanning the entire width of the stage, the set included two towers down-left and down-right, a 20-foot-wide staircase in the center of the stage, and a massive upper level. Unfortunately, with the exception of the opening scene and a few moments scattered throughout the play, the director chose to isolate the action almost completely on the downstage third of the space. Scenic designers spend countless hours of research and work to provide a show with just the right set to complement and support everything that needs to occur. As the director, you *must* use the entire space with which you are provided.

131

Keeping in mind the form and function dictum mentioned above, study the designs you are given so that you can utilize the set in its entirety. Some directors shy away from extreme upstage or side acting areas in their blocking because they are afraid of running into poor sightlines for their audience. While you certainly have to take sightlines into consideration, trust that your designers have done the same, and will be able to showcase the actors no matter the area into which you've blocked them. If you are unsure about a certain section of the set, talk with your scenic designers to make sure you know which areas are considered truly "actable."

When creating your blocking for the set, take into consideration movement and traffic patterns. With each scene, make certain you know where actors have to enter and exit, and where they have to move within each scene to accomplish the textual necessities. Once you have all of those elements covered (the function), begin to consider how you can have the actors do that in a creative, interesting, and artistic fashion (the form). Figure 9.3 shows an example of a large set being used *completely*.

Providing a "snapshot moment" of a different type, this image from *Zorro!* shows a masterful use of the entire space created by the scenic designer. Notice how the director has made use of almost every area and level, creating groupings downstage, centerstage, on the stairs and platforms, and even in the up-right cupola. The actors are all throwing their focus to the most important aspect of the scene, our hero kissing our heroine. The one spot not utilized in the image is the stage-left platforming, but you see the prone body of the defeated villain on the steps, which the director has chosen to isolate from the rest of the characters: one image, a great picture, and a great use of the space.

3. Implied within the concept of using the entire space is the idea of using depth in your blocking. In 2003, the TV show *Arrested Development* was hailed as revolutionary for eschewing the traditional three-camera set-up for television comedies. Instead,

Figure 9.3 The finale of *Zorro!* (Photo courtesy of Mark D. Guinn and the Louisiana Tech University Department of Theatre.)

it employed a single, often hand-held camera. The critical and popular success the producers of that show enjoyed led others to follow suit, with shows like *30 Rock*, *The Office*, *Community*, and *Modern Family* employing the same format. The popularity of those series bled over into theatrical staging, with many directors attempting to create the same feel with their blocking. In doing so, however, all of the action is pushed downstage center, to provide the "in your face" style of the single-camera comedy.

Unfortunately, what works on television is not always as successful in live theatre. As a medium, theatre depends on providing the audience with panorama, vista, and horizon ... which aren't necessarily a part of TV storytelling. When blocking your show, you must take into consideration the fact that you are working in a three-dimensional form, and use that to your advantage. The depth of your staging allows the audience to appreciate the fullness of the space and will create a richer and better developed look for your show.

While Figure 9.4 clearly features a single actor, both with placement and lighting, notice how the scene is rounded out

Figure 9.4 An image from *Smoke on the Mountain Homecoming*, the company of Theatre Tuscaloosa's 2010 production. (Photo courtesy of Porfirio Solorzano, Tina Turley, and Theatre Tuscaloosa.)

with the placement of the other actors. By using a variety of horizontal planes and the full depth available on the set, this moment of the show is both intimate and expansive. This type of three-dimensional sculpting draws the audience in, while allowing them to experience the fullness of the scene.

4. Also implied within the concept of using the entire space is the use of levels. Breaking up the horizontal plane and blocking with the entire depth of the stage is great, but pulling the audience's eye up and down a variety of vertical planes is just as important, if not more so. Part of understanding the full space available to you as a director is realizing that you can work left to right, front to back, and low to high. Levels are wonderful for isolating important moments and setting off characters in key scenes.

Figure 9.5, from *The Last Night of Ballyhoo*, shows the use of both depth and height to set apart Lala's entrance from everything else that is happening in the scene. Eager to display her gown, patterned after Scarlett O'Hara's in *Gone With the Wind*, Lala needs to "make an entrance," both in the literal

Figure 9.5 Lala's Appearance in *The Last Night of Ballyhoo*. (L–R: Johnny Marley, Courtney VanEaton, Ashley Davis, Kaitlin Fouquet, Kevin Keeler, Maggie McAdams, and Trey Clark. Photo courtesy of Mark D. Guinn and the Louisiana Tech University Department of Theatre.)

and figurative sense. By having her blocked, not only to enter the scene at the top of the stairs but to pause on the level and force everyone to look at her, this moment provides a great example of how vertical planes can be used advantageously.

5. Finally, when blocking your show, go back and remember the third "rule" from Chapter 3: *tell the story*. Make sure you are clear with your blocking as to who you are featuring in each scene, where the audience's eye will travel, and how the blocking supports what is happening in the scene. If you are unsure about a section of blocking and whether or not it is featuring the right person, try this trick: while sitting in the house (or rehearsal hall), close your eyes and listen to the action for a moment. When you get to the portion you want to check, open your eyes. Where does your eye immediately travel? On whom do you focus? The chances are, wherever your eye goes, is where your audience will primarily be looking. That will help tell you if you've made a good blocking choice. Also, make sure you are using the design of the production to your advantage.

In Figure 9.6, notice how the director makes use of the scenic and lighting designs. The story being told in the scene is the end of the lead character's life, and the audience sees

Figure 9.6 The finale of *W;t*, showing Dr Vivian Bearing's final appearance. (Rebecca Taylor. Photo courtesy of Mark D. Guinn and the Louisiana Tech University Department of Theatre.)

her body, ravaged by cancer, in silhouette as she disrobes one last time. It's an excellent melding of blocking and design working together to tell the story, which is your primary and ultimate goal.

Blocking Notation

As with so much of what you will eventually do as a director, you will gradually develop your own method of notating your blocking. When you sit down with your script to begin what many call your "pre-blocking" (putting the blocking you envision in your script prior to working on it with your cast), your biggest challenge is to make sure that however you decide to notate it, it is clear and understandable to you once you get to it in rehearsal. As you do put your blocking in your script, it's important to remind yourself that it may very well change once you have actors moving around space on their feet. What works in your mind and on the page often becomes a bit of a mess in real life. Flexibility is, once again, key. Be willing and able to make adjustments to your blocking as you are going through it with the cast. This is also another great example of why you need an excellent stage manager. As blocking changes are made on the fly, and you later get to a working rehearsal, actors will invariably have a question about their blocking, and what you have in your script (your original pre-blocking) may no longer be relevant. Having a great stage manager alleviates that problem.

There are generally two schools of thought on blocking. One involves being ultra-specific and dictating every single move to the actors; instructing them, for example: "Enter stage left on this line, cross down-right four steps, look over your left shoulder and say your line at that point." The other type is more *laissez faire*, and sounds like this: "Enter stage left here. By the time you get to this line, just make sure you're in the down-right corner. You figure out how you get there." There are gradations and variations, but these are the two generalities of style. While one is not demonstrably better than the other, I typically teach to err on the side of the latter if working with an experienced cast. Allowing your actors the creativity to take part in the blocking process helps them as they build their characters. Generally, the less experienced the actor, the more detailed you will have to be in your blocking.

As referenced above, every director has his or her own method of notating the blocking. On the website, you will find two different blocking forms, and we'll examine both here. Both are good foundational approaches, with one being more detailed than the other. With each, the physical manner in which you use the form in your script is the same. You will want to have your script typed or blown up and copied, so that it fits in a three-ring binder. Your blocking sheets should be opposite from a page of text (if working with an electronic version of your script, then you will want to set up a two-page view so that your blocking can be on one side of the screen and the text on the other). The first notation method is the "A—A—E" style.

1. *Action—Adjustment—Expectation.* You notice that the first blocking notation sheet is divided into three columns, labeled "action," "adjustment," and "expectation." You will use a number or symbol in the margins of your script, and then a corresponding symbol on the A—A—E sheet. In the first column, "action," you merely put the action for that character at that moment. In the "adjustment" column, you are noting any physical and/or vocal adjustment you want from the actor at that point (e.g. "pointing vigorously" or "screaming defiantly"). Your final column, "expectation," is basically the "why" of your blocking. In this column, you are putting your reason for this move. This column forces you really to think about your blocking and helps ensure that you have a strong purpose for each move. If you can't figure out something for this final column, that's a good indication that you might need to rethink that particular piece of blocking.

137

   Figures 9.7 and 9.8 show an example of a page of blocking using the A—A—E approach. Note that some common abbreviations are used:

   - X = "cross"
   - U = "up"
   - D = "down"
   - R = "right"
   - L = "left"
   - C = "center"
   - NTR = "enter"
   - XT = "exit"

So, XDR would mean, "cross down-right," etc.

   In Figures 9.7 and 9.8, you see that the director has used letters to indicate where, on the script page, blocking should happen. The corresponding letters on the notation chart show

ACT I--SCENE I. Rome. A street.   A. As lights come up.   B. A beat later
Enter FLAVIUS, MARULLUS, and certain Commoners

FLAVIUS
Hence! home, you idle creatures get you home: C.
Is this a holiday? what! know you not,
Being mechanical, you ought not walk
Upon a labouring day without the sign
Of your profession? Speak, what trade art thou?

First Commoner
Why, sir, a carpenter.

MARULLUS   D.
Where is thy leather apron and thy rule?
What dost thou with thy best apparel on?
You, sir, what trade are you?

Second Commoner
Truly, sir, in respect of a fine workman, I am but, as you would say, a cobbler.

MARULLUS
But what trade art thou? answer me directly.

Second Commoner   E.
A trade, sir, that, I hope, I may use with a safe conscience; which is, indeed, sir, a mender of bad soles.

MARULLUS   F.
What trade, thou knave? thou naughty knave, what trade?

138   **Second Commoner**
Nay, I beseech you, sir, be not out with me: yet, if you be out, sir, I can mend you.

MARULLUS   G.
What meanest thou by that? mend me, thou saucy fellow!

Second Commoner
Why, sir, cobble you.

FLAVIUS
Thou art a cobbler, art thou?   H.

Second Commoner
Truly, sir, all that I live by is with the awl: I meddle with no tradesman's matters, nor women's matters, but with awl. I am, indeed, sir, a surgeon to old shoes; when they are in great danger, I recover them. As proper men as ever trod upon neat's leather have gone upon my handiwork.

FLAVIUS
But wherefore art not in thy shop today?
Why dost thou lead these men about the streets?

Second Commoner   I.
Truly, sir, to wear out their shoes, to get myself into more work. But, indeed, sir, we make holiday, to see Caesar and to rejoice in his triumph.

Figure 9.7 Sample script page from *Julius Caesar*.

A-A-E Blocking Notation Sheet

Action	Adjustment	Expectation
A. 1st & 2nd Commoners NTR UR with wine. 3rd & 4th Commoners NTR DL with wine	A. 1 & 2 XDL to meet 3 & 4.	A. Greeting each other to celebrate.
B. F & M NTR UL	B. XC to intercept 1 & 2	B. Not happy with celebration
C. Flavius stop #1. #2 stops with him. #3 & 4 quickly XT DR.	C. Flavius take wine from #1.	C. Flavius and Marullus not happy. 1&2 drunk, but worried. 3&4 scared on XT.
D. Marullus slap # 1 on the head	D. #1 react.	D. Showing dominance
E. #2 XDR	E. Putting on a show	E. Trying to escape
F. Marullus follow #2	F. Grab his arm	F. Continue to assert self
G. Marullus grab 2's ear	G. Grab & twist. 2 React. Should be comedic	G. Wring information from him
H. Flavius XDR towards them	H. Only halfway	H. Intrigued by this guy
I. #2 XDC	I. Pluck back wine flask on the way.	I. Not realizing threat. Enjoying attention.

Figure 9.8 Sample of A—A—E blocking notation.

what is happening at that moment. The director has each column of the page filled, indicating which actors are moving, what they are doing, and the purpose behind the move. The A—A—E approach is detailed and meticulous and is an excellent tool for working with young and less experienced casts, because it helps you anticipate the "why am I doing this?" question from actors.

2. *Movement chart.* The second style, which is more general that the A—A—E method, is simply called a "movement chart." For this notation, you will need to have a copy of the groundplan for the scene on the page facing the text. Many directors like to shrink it down, so that they can get two groundplans on each page. The copy of this notation sheet found on the website is divided top and bottom, so you can put two copies of the groundplan on the page. Some directors like to photocopy (or cut and paste, if working electronically), while some directors simply like to sketch in the groundplan in pencil.

When working with this approach, you will assign each character in the scene a color. Using simple arrows, you indicate where each character should move at the appropriate time. To avoid confusion, where possible, it is best to use the same color for principal characters throughout the play. Minor characters, or groups, can use same colors or repeat colors. For example, you could assign all "soldiers/messengers/commoners" the color green. Then, each time a character of that type appears in a scene, you will assign that character the color green on your sheet. Whichever way you choose to employ it, make sure you are specific when assigning colors to each of the characters in the scene.

Figures 9.9 and 9.10 show an example of using a movement chart for blocking notation, with the same page from *Julius Caesar.* There are still letters in the script, which correspond with letters and movements on the chart, but notice that moments "D" and "G" are only notated in the script and not on the sheet. The movement chart is just that ... movements only. Specialized bits are noted in the script, and motivations and adjustments are left up to the actors, or left to discussions in the working rehearsals. The movement chart approach to blocking works great with experienced actors who are able to contribute more to the collaborative process and don't need as much specific direction.

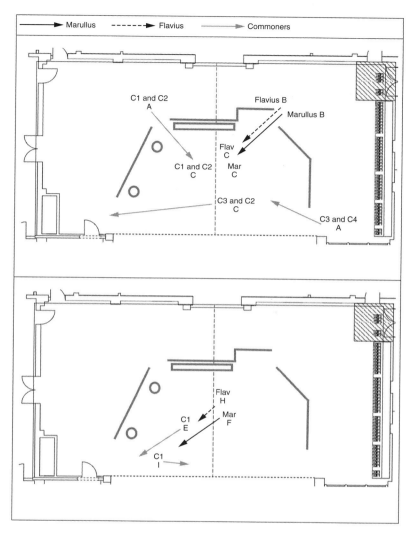

Figure 9.9 Sample of movement chart blocking notation.

Whichever approach you use when notating your blocking, you will need to know that, as mentioned before, it is likely to change once you begin working with the actors on their feet … and that's OK. Theatre is a living, breathing organism and will naturally evolve throughout the process—both in rehearsals and in performances. That's what makes it such a wonderful medium.

ACT I--SCENE I. Rome. A street.   A. As lights come up.   B. A beat later
Enter FLAVIUS, MARULLUS, and certain Commoners

FLAVIUS
Hence! home, you idle creatures get you home: C.
Is this a holiday? what! know you not,
Being mechanical, you ought not walk
Upon a labouring day without the sign
Of your profession? Speak, what trade art thou?

First Commoner
Why, sir, a carpenter.

MARULLUS   D. Slap C1's head
Where is thy leather apron and thy rule?
What dost thou with thy best apparel on?
You, sir, what trade are you?

Second Commoner
Truly, sir, in respect of a fine workman, I am but, as you would say, a cobbler.

MARULLUS
But what trade art thou? answer me directly.

Second Commoner   E.
A trade, sir, that, I hope, I may use with a safe conscience; which is, indeed, sir, a mender of bad soles.

MARULLUS   F.
What trade, thou knave? thou naughty knave, what trade?

Second Commoner
Nay, I beseech you, sir, be not out with me: yet, if you be out, sir, I can mend you.

MARULLUS   G. Grab C2's ear
What meanest thou by that? mend me, thou saucy fellow!

Second Commoner
Why, sir, cobble you.

FLAVIUS
Thou art a cobbler, art thou?   H.

Second Commoner
Truly, sir, all that I live by is with the awl: I meddle with no tradesman's matters, nor women's matters, but with awl. I am, indeed, sir, a surgeon to old shoes; when they are in great danger, I recover them. As proper men as ever trod upon neat's leather have gone upon my handiwork.

FLAVIUS
But wherefore art not in thy shop today?
Why dost thou lead these men about the streets?

Second Commoner   I.
Truly, sir, to wear out their shoes, to get myself into more work. But, indeed, sir, we make holiday, to see Caesar and to rejoice in his triumph.

Figure 9.10 Sample script page of *Julius Caesar*.

Exercises and Suggested Reading

Exercises

For the following exercises, use Act I, scene ii of Shakespeare's *Julius Caesar*. Create a basic groundplan for your set. Each student can either create his or her own groundplan or the class can create one as a whole.

1. Use the Action—Adjustment—Expectation chart from the website and notate blocking for *Julius Caesar*, Act I, scene ii. Make sure to have the chart on a page facing the script pages, with your movement moments notated both in the script and on the chart.
2. Use the movement chart from the website and notate blocking for *Julius Caesar*, Act I, scene ii. Use the same basic blocking you devised for Exercise 1, but remember that certain moments will be notated in the script and not on the chart.

Notes

1. Charles Marowitz, *Directing the Action: Acting and Directing in the Contemporary Theatre* (New York: Applause Theatre Book Publishers, 1986), 56.
2. Arthur Bartow, "Douglas Turner Ward," in *The Director's Voice, Twenty-One Interviews* (New York: Theatre Communications Group, Inc., 1988), 304.
3. Tennessee Williams, *Camino Real* (New York: New Directions, 2008), xxxiv.
4. Arthur Bartow, "Des McAnuff," in *The Director's Voice, Twenty-One Interviews* (New York: Theatre Communications Group, Inc., 1988), 220.
5. Anne Bogart, *A Director Prepares—Seven Essays on Art and Theatre* (New York: Routledge, 2005), 134.
6. Deborah Saivetz, *An Event in Space: JoAnne Akalaitis in Rehearsal* (Hanover, NH: Smith and Krauss, Inc., 2000), 123.

Suggested Reading

Congreve, William. *The Way of the World* (c.1700, available online).

Coward, Noël. *Hay Fever* (New York: Samuel French, 2014 (1924)).

Edson, Margaret. *W;t* (New York: Dramatists Play Service, 1999).

Gorky, Maxim. *The Lower Depths* (1901–1902, available online).

Ray, Connie, Bailey, Alan, and Craver, Mike. *Smoke on the Mountain Homecoming* (New York: Samuel French, 2012).

Richmond, David. *Zorro!* (Adapted from Johnston MCulley, *The Curse of Capistrano*, originally serialized 1919, available online).

Shakespeare, William. *Julius Caesar* (*c.*1599, available online).

Shakespeare, William. *King John* (1623, available online).

Shakespeare, William. *Richard II* (*c.*1595, available online).

Uhry, Alfred. *The Last Night of Ballyhoo* (New York: Dramatists Play Service, 1997).

Wilder, Thornton. *Our Town* (New York: Samuel French, 2010 (1938)).

Williams, Tennessee. *Camino Real* (New York: New Directions, 2008 (1953)).

144

CHAPTER 10

Working and Running

Some directors love the research and conceptualizing that leads up to a production. Some directors love the collaboration of the design process. Still other directors love the reveal of opening a show to an audience. But not all directors love all of those things. The one area of a production, though, that every director I have ever known really *loves*, is working and running rehearsals. This is the time that you get to put the show on its feet, see it grow and develop, collaborate with the actors, and watch them bring the characters to life. It is an exciting, frustrating, challenging, thrilling, terrifying, and joyous time. These are the rehearsals where the show is fleshed out and all of the collaborators get to breathe life into the production.

Working Rehearsals

Having made it this far into the book, it should come as no surprise to you that there are a wide variety of ways to conduct working rehearsals. In general, however, your working rehearsals will fall into two categories (or timeframes): on-book rehearsals; and off-book rehearsals. A lot of similar work happens during each timeframe/ category, but the difference often lies in the depth or amount of work.

On-Book Rehearsals

Once your show is blocked and you start on your working rehearsals, the first thing you are likely to discover is how much of your blocking *doesn't* work (cheery thought, right?). The nature of blocking almost guarantees that there will be elements that don't hold together the farther into the process you get. You begin with your pre-blocking when it's just you and the script; that begins to alter once you have actual actors with whom to work; and the alteration naturally continues once the actors begin working with the blocking on a regular basis. Sometimes you will discover positions and traffic patterns that are awkward or don't work right away, but often it's a gradual process of discovery on the part of the actors as they move along the path of bringing the characters to life. Much of these first working rehearsals will be dedicated to fine-tuning your blocking.

Just as we talked about in the previous chapter, you have to be flexible with your direction. If you enter the rehearsal period understanding that things are likely to change, it will make it that much easier to accept and *participate* in the change. I once adjudicated a production of James Goldman's *The Lion in Winter*, where the actors were interesting, the set and costumes were beautiful, the sound design was fantastic ... but the blocking was awkward and stiff. After the show, I mentioned that to someone I knew who was on faculty where the play was produced. She told me that the young director had blocked the show in the rehearsal studio and impressed upon the actors not to vary *one bit* from the blocking they had been given. The director's unyielding position on his blocking wound up hurting what otherwise would have been a very fine production.

As you start working with the actors on their feet, they will be getting used to their traffic patterns and finding what does and does not work for them. Sometimes there may be technical reasons for needing to adjust blocking—for example, the coffee table the scenic designer has found to use is larger than you anticipated and that cramps traffic patterns on its downstage side. Sometimes there may be what I call "actor" reasons—for example, the actor can't find a way to justify a certain cross or position and comes to you with a suggestion for a change. Whatever the reason, you need to be open to the possibility of change and then willing to engage in the discovery of a solution. You should also understand that you may not find the solution right away. Whether it's adjusting the traffic patterns of blocking or rearranging a stage picture you've created, it may take several tries; you might even find that you need to leave a moment alone for a few rehearsals and then come back to it later.

Eventually, you will discover that the blocking seems to be working for everyone (you and the actors) and you can move on to working with your actors on character development...

146

Allow me to diverge here for just a moment. I am presenting these periods of rehearsal in a somewhat linear and cut-and-dried form for the purposes of this book. The reality is that many of these periods will overlap, coincide, and otherwise commingle. Character development goes on at the same time as fine-tuning blocking, and so on. But for clarity's sake, here on the printed page, we address them individually. Now, back to our scheduled paragraph.

Encourage your actors to work in these rehearsals with a pencil at the ready. Because they have their scripts in hands, they should have all of their blocking, notes, and questions scribbled throughout. And when they make a new discovery, or when you provide a particularly brilliant directorial insight, they will want to jot that down in the margins of their script. As you begin the rehearsal period, you are going to know more about the characters than the actors do. However, that should change over the coming days and weeks. The more the actors do their homework and dig into their roles, the more they are going to take the lead in the development of their characters. These working rehearsals, with scripts in hand, are the time for you to help shape and guide their character growth.

"Guiding character growth" is one of those things that is much easier said than done. There is a tightrope that you, as a director, have to walk with actors, balancing between the need to communicate your vision and the need to allow them the creativity to explore and *play*. You certainly begin the rehearsal process with a strong vision of what each character should be, and you must understand that the actor does as well. Your task is to find a way to shape and guide the actor's development of character without dictating every little thing. One of the best ways you can do this is by asking questions—and asking *one* question specifically. We'll get to the *one* question in a moment, but first let's examine some general questions you can ask to help your actors.

In her seminal book *Respect for Acting*, Uta Hagen points out that some actors have difficulty connecting to a character because they can't "find themselves" in it:

Someone working on Laura in *The Glass Menagerie* will state flatly, "But I've never been shy." I have only to suggest a time when she may have been to a high school dance with a big pimple on her chin, and the memory will turn the unshy actress into a blushing wallflower.[1]

The simple question that Hagen asks the actress immediately unlocks a connection to the character. Listening to what actors are having difficulty with and then asking leading or probing questions to get them thinking on another track can be hugely beneficial in helping them connect the dots.

Another great technique is to turn actors' questions around on them. I was once in a production of Tennessee Williams' *Summer and Smoke* and asked the director just how awkward the character needed to be. He simply looked at me and said, "Well, what do you think?" The director recognized that the impetus for my question lay in my own uncertainty and a desire to be told what to do. He also correctly surmised that I needed the confidence to explore my own choices. By making me think about it and talk my way through it, he allowed me to take creative ownership of the role, while still ensuring that the character was moving in a direction that fit in with his overall vision of the play.

Now we come to that *one* magical question ... Assume you are directing a production of Pearl Cleage's *Flyin' West*, and are doing scene work in rehearsal. While working, you notice that the actress playing Fannie (who is one of the characters who was *not* born into slavery) is jumping straight into her relationship with Wil (one of the characters who *was* born into slavery). You don't want to stifle the building rapport and chemistry between the two characters, but you do want Fannie to be a little more stand-offish and perhaps even haughty toward Wil when they first meet. So, to guide the actress along, you ask, "What would happen if you weren't so sure about Wil to begin with?" By employing the "what would happen if...?" question, you are engaging the actress and getting her thinking about exploring possibilities without quashing or dismissing the choices she is already making. As you both investigate the various answers to the question, you will begin to find the best developmental path for the character, and eventually arrive at a place that both satisfies the creative needs of the actor and helps develop the overall continuity of the production.

"What would happen if...?" is not only a great question for character development, but also for blocking, physicalization, vocal work, etc. It is merely an extension of the idea of communication and respect that we discussed earlier in the book. As is so often the case with directing (and, really, most professions), maintaining an ongoing dialogue is typically much more beneficial than dictatorial orders.

Off-Book Rehearsals

Eventually, and often to the dismay of actors, you have to move to rehearsing without a net—the dreaded off-book rehearsals. Every actor has his or her own method for getting off-book, and student actors spend a lot of time figuring out which method works best for them. While you can certainly assist the process of learning lines, it's ultimately something the actor has to do on his or her own. The biggest temptation you have to avoid when directing is enabling the actors by giving them "just one more day" to have their script in their pocket and pull it out to check it "for just a minute." You will eventually have to pull the plug on them and let them sink or swim.

As a disclaimer, I should point out that most of this section does *not* refer to working with professional actors. The majority of professional acting contracts, both Equity and non-Equity, require actors to be off-book when they show up for the first day of rehearsals. Some actors are more successful than others at this, but, by and large it's not really something with which you have to concern yourself as a director. The main downside to working this way is breaking any vocal habits or patterns the actors may have developed when learning their lines.

With the companies and shows that most young directors start out working with, you will have to manage the process of getting actors off-book. As mentioned above, you can assist the transition to working without a script for the actors, and the best way to do this is to break the show into sections. Instead of having the first off-book rehearsal be a run-through of the entire show, you will find the going much easier if you do an off-book rehearsal for Act I on one day, and Act II the next. Some directors even break it down by scenes. When you schedule your off-book rehearsals, don't try to accomplish anything else that day. In Chapter 8, we talked about scheduling rehearsals and the importance of specifying what you are hoping to accomplish in each rehearsal when you make out the schedule. For your initial off-book rehearsals, your rehearsal goals and evaluation sheet will only have one entry: "work off-book for first time."

If you've ever been in (or involved with) a show, you know that the first off-book rehearsals can be a painful process. Make sure your actors know that you are not expecting perfection; they are most likely putting enough pressure on themselves, so try not to add to it. Let them know that the goal is for them to be on their feet and working off-book. Encourage them to remember what they've worked on up to that point, but this rehearsal should really just be about remembering words. Understand too, this will probably be a bit of trainwreck, depending on the experience level of your actors. Let it happen. Let them go through the process, with encouragement and as much good humour as you can muster. They will get there and you'll be able to move on to deeper work.

Once your actors are off-book, you pick back up with your working rehearsals where you focus on character growth, finding the arcs, making choices, and discovering the rhythm and flow of the show. At this point in the rehearsal, directions taken and choices made are beginning to be refined, honed, and deepened by the actors. Founding director of the Open Space Theatre Charles Marowitz calls this process "activation." Making a comparison between actors and musicians, and using an idea from the conductor, Otto Klemperer, Marowitz says, "Once the notion behind a scene has been insinuated and the dynamics suggested, it is the act of actors 'breathing naturally' ... that fulfills or frustrates the director's design."[2] The actors are now *activating* their characters, to use Marowitz's term.

In order to help the actors activate their characters, your work with them shifts a little bit from what it was when you were working on-book. At this point in the rehearsal process, you should be watching, listening, and offering suggestions here and there. This is when the actors are doing the most work on developing their roles, and *over*-direction is a quick way to confuse them or stifle their growth. I was once in a production of Horton Foote's *The Trip to Bountiful* and we were working off-book. As we finished a particularly emotional scene, the director sidled up to me and said very quietly, "That was great. Try it again, and this time, more yellow." *More yellow*. Perhaps the vaguest direction ever given to an actor, but it was the absolute perfect suggestion to give to me at that time. I immediately knew he liked the way I was playing the scene, but wanted it a little bit lighter and a little bit brighter. We restarted the scene and I was able to find the perfect texture and rhythm for the character. A simple suggestion from the director allowed me to activate the character in exactly the way that was needed in that moment.

Running Rehearsals

After working through the show with the actors off-book, you then progress to run-throughs of the show. This period in the rehearsal process, prior to adding technical elements, is when you begin to pull back from stopping and starting and working directly. The actors are allowed to run the show, while you watch and note it. At this point, your cast is beginning to get a feel for the true pacing and rhythm of the show, and you will be taking notes on a wide variety of topics, from blocking to character to vocal work to pacing to arc. During these rehearsals, Anne Bogart comments that the "biggest contribution to a production, and the only real gift [you] can offer an actor, is [your] attention. What counts most is the quality of [your] attention."[3] You must be *present* and you must be *attentive* so that the notes you take can be as beneficial as possible to your actors.

Setting up your goals and evaluations for working rehearsals, technical rehearsals, and dress rehearsals is relatively easy. The things that need work are usually pretty obvious. That is not necessarily the case in your running rehearsals. It's easy to get lost in running rehearsals and you find yourself either trying to look at too much or not looking at enough. Because of this, it's more important than ever for you to specify your goals for each rehearsal. Don't try to take notes on everything at once; instead, identify areas on which you want to focus in rehearsal and note those. You will find that if you go into the rehearsal with a specific idea of what you want to watch for, taking notes during the rehearsal will be much simpler.

Through trial and error, you will discover the way you take notes best. Some directors like to use a notepad and pencil; some use a laptop, tablet or other mobile device; some like to dictate their notes to an assistant. Whichever method you employ, the most important thing is to make sure your notes are understandable ... to you. One of the most frustrating things—for actors and directors—is to sit in notes after rehearsal and have the time extended while the director tries to decipher each note. Whether it's illegible (if handwritten) or cryptic, unclear notes are a huge time-waster. Your notes should be clear, precise, and (hopefully!) insightful.

When giving notes to your actors, it's vital that you understand what works best for each individual. Each actor responds differently. Some might listen and write down their notes, while asking the occasional question for clarity. Some actors want to discuss every note given, offering suggestions, clarifications, or (unfortunately, in some cases) excuses. I once worked with a brilliant actress who was about 5'1" tall. The first night I gave notes to the cast, all she did was stare at me ... hard ... violently (can a stare be "violent?" Somehow, this was). Looking at her watch me as I gave her notes, Shakespeare's lines, spoken by Helena in *Midsummer*, came to mind: "Oh, when she's angry, she is keen and shrewd!/She was a vixen when she went to school./And though she be but little, she is fierce."[4] I honestly worried that she might explode at some point. The next rehearsal, she not only implemented every single note that I had given the night before, but she had improved and built on them tremendously. I realized that her intense stares weren't malicious at all; she was merely concentrating and soaking in every note I gave her so that she could go home and work on them before the next rehearsal. Although you may not work with an actor who responds to notes in that specific way, you will encounter many different types of actor and should be prepared to give notes in a variety of ways.

One aspect of note-giving that most young directors have trouble with is how to handle that moment when one of your actors seems not to take a note or not to be able to implement it. When an actor doesn't take a note, you must remember that *it is always your fault*. Perhaps "fault" is not the best word to use here, since laying blame isn't particularly helpful, but putting it like that helps you remember that communication is *your* responsibility. Assume you're directing a production of William Inge's *Picnic*, and noting Act 3, scene i between Howard and Rosemary. The scene involves schoolteacher Rosemary trying to hold her boyfriend Howard to his promise to marry her. After going back and forth with each other throughout the scene, Howard briefly agrees to marriage the next morning, before quickly reconsidering: "No. I'm not gonna marry anyone that says, 'You gotta marry me Howard,' I'm not gonna. If a woman wants me to marry her … she could at least say 'please.' "[5]

After watching the run, you feel that the actor playing Howard is being too heavy-handed with those final lines, and is missing the comedy. So, you give him the note to lighten up on those lines. The next rehearsal comes around and you see that the actor is playing the line exactly the same way. Remember, fight the urge to blame the actor for not taking the note! This first time, you should simply give the note again. While it may be true that he simply forgot it (and most actors, when a note is given the second time because they forgot, will own up to forgetting), it's your job to ensure he understands what you want out of the moment. If you get to the next rehearsal and he still hasn't taken the note, then you need to figure out a different way to give it. Perhaps this time, you get more specific, saying, "This moment is playing too serious right now. See what you can do to play the comedy of it more." Now you get to the next rehearsal, and he is *still* missing the comedy and playing it too seriously (this is a common occurrence with young actors playing this role). It's your job to find yet another way to give the note to try and achieve what the scene needs.

At some point, actors realize that they are simply not getting it and they know that you are giving the same note (essentially) again and again. Trust me, they feel awful about it and are working to give you what you want. This is where your willingness to take responsibility becomes even more important, because you can easily break an actor's spirit if you pound and pound a note. When I start to sense that an actor is feeling a bit beaten down but I still want to give the note, I try once more, but preface the note with, "I'm sorry. I've done a really poor job of communicating on this. Let me see if I can do it better..." By taking responsibility for communicating the note, you are letting the actor know that you recognize the communal and collaborative nature of what you're doing, and easing a bit of the pressure. It might even be beneficial at this point to suggest a discussion with the actor outside of rehearsal, where you can go over things in more depth, without the pressure of the entire cast waiting while you give notes to one actor.

153

Unfortunately, there will usually be moments in every show where, no matter how many times or ways you give a note, you just can't seem to get your point across to one of your actors. When this occurs (and it will), you will have to make a decision to either "fish or cut bait." In other words, you may just need to recognize that the actor is giving you everything he or she has. If you have attempted multiple times to give the same note to no avail, then you have to understand that you've hit a point of diminishing returns. If you continue banging your head against that metaphorical wall, you will then wind up ignoring other aspects of the show that need your attention. Continuing to give the same note over and over (albeit in different ways), will just frustrate everyone involved and stymie the growth that is still possible with the show.

Way back in Chapter 2, we talked about the importance of understanding the needs of different types of actor with whom you will work (the "kick 'em in the butt or pat 'em on the butt" protocol). The note-taking and note-giving process is where this knowledge is most beneficial for you. For some actors, your notes can be esoteric and intellectual; for some, you can be direct and practical; and for some, you will need to couch the note almost as a request that you'd like the actor to consider. Actors all find a way of approaching things that works for them, and rarely are two actors the same. As you get a feel for your cast, you will discover which approach works best for which actor.

Because you will work with so many different personality types, it will be to your benefit to develop the ability to give notes in a wide variety of ways. The one thing you should always bear in mind for every note you give is the inherent fragility of the creative process. We teach actors that the rehearsal hall is a safe place where they are allowed to explore, be vulnerable, make choices, and … fail. We *want* actors to experiment and try new things in rehearsal, but the quickest way to squash those creative possibilities is by giving a note that is deprecatory, demeaning, or harsh in some manner. To avoid those spirit-crushing notes, pay close attention to the way that you phrase your comments. Ask questions when possible, and find positives to build on. Remind actors that notes are not a personal affront, and their purpose is to assist the actor in giving the strongest possible performance. Below are some phrases that you can use when giving notes; the idea behind them is that, by thinking about the *way* you give a note, the meaning behind the note will be more clear and useful.

- What would happen if you try…?
- Would it feel better/make more sense/work better/be easier if you…?
- Think about…
- Have you considered…?
- I like _____, could you now add _____?

In addition to phrases like that, embrace the collaborative spirit and ask actors for their ideas. Quite frankly, there will be times that you aren't sure *what* the right note is … you just know that a moment isn't working. Don't be afraid to say that to your actors, "This moment isn't quite right, but I'm not sure what I would do to change it. What do you think? Does it feel right to you, or do you have other ideas you can try?" You will be surprised how often the actor, who has lived with the character day and night, will have just the right idea to make it work!

Before wrapping up this section and moving onto the next phase of rehearsals, I should mention a time in rehearsals that every single director goes through, and no-one likes. Exactly when this phenomenon occurs varies from show to show, but it is typically sometime during a series of run-throughs—after being off-book for a bit, but before moving to technical rehearsals. I call this period of rehearsals "Holy crap nothing's working; this is horrible; why did I ever think I could do this?!" Unfortunately, there always seems to be a natural lull in the rehearsal calendar when the show just doesn't seem to be working. Sometimes it's because of low energy or poor pacing from the cast during a run. Sometimes it's due to uneven characters or rhythm. Sometimes you can't exactly put your finger on a reason, but you just know that the show seems *off* in some way. It's important to recognize that this happens in every show and you will come through it on the other side. It may only last one rehearsal, or as many as three or four, but it will pass. As a director, fight the tendency and desire to over-direct at this point. While there may be specific moments you can work on and fix, trust that on the whole the show doesn't need "fixing." Encourage your actors to keep living in their scripts and keep working on making discoveries, and you will soon find you move past this awful phase, and are ready to embark on the next chapter of the rehearsal process (and of this book!).

Exercises and Suggested Reading

Exercise

1. As you did in Chapter 9, use Act I, scene ii from Shakespeare's *Julius Caesar*. Working in groups, take turns with each member of your group serving as director and each serving as one of the actors. Go through the blocking and a few basic working rehearsals. Have a rehearsal where you run the scene (on or off-book) and give notes to your actors. After you have each had the opportunity to direct the scene, discuss with each other the direction, suggestions, and notes that each provided as director. What worked for you as an actor? What was more difficult to grasp? Was there one style or approach that stood out as most beneficial? Share your findings with the class.

Notes

1. Uta Hagen, *Respect for Acting* (New York, MacMillan Publishing Company, 1973), 29.

2. Charles Marowitz, *Directing the Action* (New York: Applause Theatre Book Publishers, 1986), 56.

3. Uta Hagen, *Respect for Acting* (New York: MacMillan, 1979 (1973)), 74.
4. William Shakespeare, *A Midsummer Night's Dream*, III, ii, 333–335.
5. William Inge, *Picnic* (New York: Dramatists Play Service, 1983), 60.

Suggested Reading

Cleage, Pearl. *Flyin' West* (New York: Dramatists Play Service, 1995).

Goldman, James. *The Lion in Winter* (New York: Samuel French, 2011 (1966)).

Hagen, Uta. *Respect for Acting* (New York: MacMillan, 1979 (1973)).

Inge, William. *Picnic* (New York: Dramatists Play Service, 1983 (1953)).

Marowitz, Charles. *Directing the Action* (Milwaukee, WI: Applause Theatre and Cinema Books, 2000 (1986)).

Williams, Tennessee. *Summer and Smoke* (New York: Dramatists Play Service, 1998 (1948)).

156

CHAPTER 11

Techs and Dresses

As you move out of the run-through phase of rehearsals, you must prepare for the technical rehearsals, dress rehearsals, and, eventually, opening night. This time in rehearsals requires a very definite shift in your focus and perspective, as you are paying less attention to the work of the actors and more attention to the shape and function of the show as a whole. Another step in this process, and one that is extremely difficult for some directors, is beginning to let go control of the show and turning it over to your PSM.

157

It is important to make sure that your actors know that, while you (of course) want them to continue to explore and grow in their characters and continue to make discoveries, the time for changes and alterations has now passed. Once you get to technical rehearsals, the framework of your show must be set—blocking, beats, stage business—all need to be at a definitive point. This is vital for your designers (who are setting cues based on the rehearsals they've watched) and your PSM (who is beginning to learn where, exactly, the cues are to be called). There is nothing that will frustrate and annoy your production team more than if you are still changing entrances and altering blocking as technical rehearsals begin. If you can't set the framework of the show, then they will never be able to learn what needs to happen, and when.

Another important point to make to your actors at this juncture is that your notes and comments will be focused much more on the technical elements, and much less on what they are doing as performers. You will still be looking at stage pictures, positioning, pacing, etc., but your focus is shifting now, and you will have to give your attention to the technical side as opposed to the acting side. Encourage actors to continue to ask questions if they need assistance with a specific moment or line, but within the rehearsal itself your attention is going to be much broader in scope. As techs come to an end and you move into dresses, that scope will begin to narrow down a bit, and your attention will gradually shift back to the performances, before broadening out completely to include the entirety of the production as you finish the rehearsals.

Tech Rehearsals

As you have seen, communication has been a running theme throughout this book, and that doesn't change now. It is vitally important for you to sit down with your designers and technical director *before rehearsals ever begin* and determine what the shape and timing of tech rehearsals will be. Most theatres structure technical rehearsals in a way that they have found works best for them, and that isn't the same in every theatre. Especially if it is your first time working with a company, designer, or TD, you will want to discuss how tech rehearsals will happen before you ever begin the rehearsal process—while you are making out your rehearsal calendar. You will want to know specifics, as the number and structure of tech rehearsals will affect how much time you have for other rehearsals. While there are a wide variety of tech rehearsal styles, they typically fall into one of two categories: definite techs or gradual techs.

Definite Techs

Definite techs are those that are scheduled for specific dates. At that point (say, March 9, just as an example) you know you will be operating with all (or most) technical elements put into the show. The set may still need paint or specific elements, but it is complete and in place. The props are complete. The lighting and sound designs, while certain cues may need to be touched up, are complete. It may be that you start by teching Act I in one rehearsal, and Act II the next, or it may be that you try to make it through the entire show in one rehearsal, but regardless, there is a hard deadline on your rehearsal calendar for techs to begin.

Gradual Techs

Gradual techs are much looser and freer with the integration of technical elements. With this approach, you will typically have a week designated for technical elements to be added in to the show as they become available. You might have certain scenic elements and a few props one night, the Act I light cues (or the designer playing with light cues) the next night, a few sound cues the next, and so on. Gradual techs don't necessarily give you a deadline on your calendar, as much as a range of rehearsals when you will begin seeing technical elements.

Though you will certainly have a style that you like better as a director, you should remember that the technical rehearsals (at least at the beginning) are more for the designers, technicians, actors, and, most importantly, stage management, than they are for you. It will be in your (and your show's) best interest to fit yourself into the type of technical rehearsal preferred by your company/TD/designers/production coordinator/PSM. These are the ones charged with making sure that everything you desire for your production happens, so you need to accommodate them. As well as variation in the general approach and timing of technical rehearsals, you will also find the shape of the actual technical rehearsal can change depending on the preferences of those involved. Some PSMs, along with design and technical crews, prefer to stop, go back, and restart until each cue or technical moment is executed perfectly (or to the PSM's satisfaction). Others would rather plow through the show, only stopping if *absolutely* necessary, and address issues with notes at the end of the rehearsal. Again, it is advisable to adapt your approach to whatever works best for your production team.

A slight diversion here to talk about paper techs and Q2Qs for a minute. Many PSMs like to have a paper tech with designers before getting into technical rehearsals. This is where the PSM sits with the designers and Go's through the script, "dry-calling" the show, to make sure that everyone knows where the cues need to happen and that warnings and goes are in the right place. A Q2Q is when the running crew goes through the show, running each and every cue (set, lights, sound, etc.) but skipping the text in between. Sometimes Q2Qs involve the actors and sometimes not. In the case of both paper techs and Q2Qs, it's best for the director to talk with the PSM and designers ahead of time to ask if you are wanted at these rehearsals. Some PSMs like to have a director present so that they can ask questions about cue placement or duration, while some prefer to go through everything on their own and then have the director give notes on what doesn't work in the actual tech rehearsal. Whichever your PSM's preference, remember that these rehearsals are *their* time, and you need to work to assist *their* needs.

The addition of technical elements into a show invariably gets a cast excited. When they see the lights, set pieces, props, etc. coming into place, the reality and closeness of opening night sets in and often kicks the actors into a new gear. What you don't want to happen, however, is for them to be thrown off by technical elements. In his definitive book for stage managers, Lawrence Stern instructs PSMs, "From the very first rehearsal, you should call every light, sound, and special-effects cue. Do this with such regularity and accuracy that no cast member ever fears for a second that you will miss a cue during the production."[1] While Stern offers this admonition to ensure that actors trust the cues will be there in performance, a side-effect is that they are getting used to the cues from the beginning of rehearsals. By doing this, the actors are much less likely to be thrown off once you actually begin technical rehearsals.

Your job as a director changes relatively drastically once tech rehearsals begin. Perhaps "job" isn't the right word as much as "focus." Bearing in mind the two tenets "tell the story" and "everything matters," you will need to pay attention to *all* the technical elements in the show, as well as when cues happen, to make certain that those two rules are being followed. For young directors, particularly those working with full production values for the first time, this can be difficult. Like most directors, I began my career in a "guerrilla theatre" style that included one or two people doing all of the jobs required and producing plays with a minimalist quality. The first show on which I worked with a full staff, a real budget, and full production values was William Inge's *Bus Stop*. The first technical rehearsal came, and we had a full set—complete with 14-foot-high walls, doors, windows, tables, chairs, stools, and a working kitchen. I was so stunned and amazed by what I was seeing that at the end of rehearsal all I could say was, "I'm sorry. I have absolutely no notes for anyone tonight. I was too busy looking at that *giant set* on the stage!" Needless to say, I was not a particularly useful director that night.

One of the first things for which you have to watch in technical rehearsals is how the actors' traffic patterns are working. No matter how assiduously your stage managers tape out the set in the rehearsal hall, actors are going to develop bad habits of "walking through walls" or "stepping off platforms." Or maybe that music stand you've been using in the rehearsal hall to represent a Christmas tree lent itself to a stage picture that just doesn't work when you get onstage with an actual Christmas tree on the set. Once there is an actual set in place, actors may find that they have unconsciously created shortcuts or adapted their blocking in some way that isn't physically possible when platforms and flats are in place. Because of this, you will have to pay close attention to the blocking and stage pictures. You may find that moments or transitions you thought were set will need to be retouched a bit to fit the reality of the set. The same holds true with any props that actors might have been pantomiming or using rehearsal props for while in the studio. Once the actual show props begin to be used, you will need to make sure they are not causing problems for the actors and that the actors are handling them in a manner consistent with the style and structure of the show. This is especially true for consumable props (food, liquid, cigarettes, etc.). Actors working with consumables for the first time will often suddenly forget how their mouths and throats work, and may need some extra time. Bearing in mind budgetary constrictions, it's important to give your actors as many run-throughs with consumables as you can.

The ethereal design elements (lights and sound) are often the most difficult for a young director to judge in a technical rehearsal. The best lighting and sound designs are subtle and supportive, complementing your direction and leading the audience's attention. The classic design textbook *Scene Design and Stage Lighting* notes that "the basic obligation of light on the stage is to give the actor or performer *meaning* in his or her surroundings and to provide an atmosphere in which the role may be logically interpreted."[2] While sound design is often more specific (a phone rings, a car door slams, etc.), the sound designer also looks to "imagine the ambient sounds that can be created to enrich the feeling of the action."[3] Sometimes even the ambient choices are dictated to the sound designer by the script. Tennessee Williams does this in many of his plays, most notably in *A Streetcar Named Desire*. As Blanche is describing, in the most melancholy terms, the young boy she loved, Williams provides stage directions to go along with Blanche's monologue:

> [*Polka music sounds, in a minor key faint with distance*]
> BLANCHE. We danced the Varsouviana! Suddenly in the middle of the dance the boy I had married broke away from me and ran out of the casino. A few moments later—a shot!
> [*Polka music stops abruptly.*]
> [*Blanche rises stiffly. Then, the polka resumes in a major key.*][4]

The purpose and effectiveness of Williams' indication of "The Varsouviana" shifting from a minor key to a major key is pretty evident. However, it's not always a simple thing to see how light is "giving a performer meaning," or to hear how sound can "enrich the feeling," even for an experienced director.

With that in mind, you really do have to pay close attention in order to notice what's happening in a given scene. Assuming that, in your design meetings, you've had discussions about needs, emotions, and the feeling of the show, then look and listen to see that those are all being met. Occasionally, you may have obvious notes to give—when, say, a cue goes in the wrong place or an actor is standing in the dark—but often you won't have such definitive things to respond to. Some things to consider when looking at and listening to your light and sound design:

- Are the lights drawing your focus away from the action?
- Are there odd shadows or "dead spots" onstage?
- If an actor is consistently in one of those dead spots, is it because of a hanging location, and do you need to adjust the blocking?
- Does the intensity (brightness) of the lights work in each scene?
- Are specials placed correctly and effectively?
- Do colors support the emotional aspect of the scene?
- Does the sound support the scene?
- Do the volume levels work in each scene?
- Is the timing and duration of sound cues effective?
- Does the sound reinforce a theme or idea?
- Does the sound seem intrusive in a scene?

Remember that, the more you direct and work with these elements, the more effectively you will be able to gauge them. If you are unsure, then go back to the rule of communication: talk with your designers and ask them if there is anything in particular they would like you to pay attention to during the rehearsal. Ask what you *should* be looking at and listening for in a given scene.

The further along you get through the technical rehearsals, the more you will need to pull back from "controlling" the rehearsal. One of the most difficult things for many directors is giving over control to the production stage manager—but you have to learn how to "let go." Mary Fran Crook, Coordinator of the Visual and Performing Arts Department and Management Professor at Grambling

162

State University, notes the importance of a director turning over rehearsals to the PSM, saying,

The stage manager is going to be controlling all aspects of the show once it gets into performance, so the earlier that can happen in rehearsal and she or he can become accustomed to it, the better. Additionally, most directors are looking at the bigger picture of the show, and won't be as knowledgeable of the technical ins and outs of the show."[5]

Because the PSM will call the show, no one (not even you) will know as much about it—how it fits together, flows, and flourishes. As we've mentioned before, you have to have trust that your stage manager is just as good at his or her job as you are, and you have to allow the PSM to do that job.

Part of allowing the PSM to do the job comes in the way in which you give notes in technical rehearsals. It's yet another thing that you will improve at with experience, but one of the biggest keys to notes during technical rehearsals is knowing *what* you are giving a note about, and, by extension, to *whom* you should give the note. For example, assume you are directing *Miss Evers' Boys*, and are giving notes during a tech rehearsal. In the scene out in the field, where Hodman is hallucinating and "killing ants," you notice that the light shift that accompanies his descent into madness is off. The questions you have to ask yourself are as follows. Is the shift happening too soon or too late? Is it taking too long or not enough time? Is the location, intensity, or color of the lights off? If the answer to either one of the first question is "yes," then you need to address your note to the PSM. If the answer to the second question is "yes," then it could be a note for the PSM or for the designer to check fade times. If the answer to the third question is "yes," then your note goes to the designer. Demonstrating a knowledge of the correct person to give the note to is a simple way to show that you respect the process and the work of your collaborators.

Respecting the work of your collaborators is always important of course, but it is vital during technical rehearsals, when patience is often in short supply and tempers can become frayed. As mentioned several times throughout this book, your communication style goes a long way toward determining the success of the process. If you are dictatorial in giving notes, demanding changes in looks or cues, you will only succeed in alienating your production team. Remember the technique of *asking questions*. Could you call that cue a line or two

163

earlier? Can this look have a bit of a cooler feel? Can we work the phone-ringing cue with the actor to get the timing down? Lead by example in the collaborative spirit and the entire process will work better for everyone involved.

Dress Rehearsals

Ideally, throughout the rehearsal period, you should periodically check in with your costume designer to see how the build is coming along. If there are specialty pieces for certain actors—a fat suit, exceptionally high heels, a hoop skirt, etc.—you may request that they have access to those pieces as soon as possible in rehearsals. If there is anything that might profoundly affect an actor's movement or characterization, you want him or her to have as many opportunities as possible to work with it. Beyond that, you typically won't get to see the actors wearing their costumes until the dress rehearsals. Though it's not the same at every theatre, you can usually count on the dress rehearsals to be broken into three parts: the costume parade, the dress rehearsals, and final dress.

Costume Parade

Sometimes called a "dress parade," the costume parade is the first opportunity you will have to see *all* the costumes in the show. It is an opportunity for you to sit with your designers and stage managers and see the actors onstage in their costumes for the first time. Not only are you looking at them and gauging fit, cut, and appropriateness, but you should also look at them under the correct lights for the scenes in which they appear, to make sure that the colors work together. The costume parade gives you the chance to have an ongoing dialogue with your designer about any changes that might need to be made before you get into the full dress rehearsals. Hem lengths, detail work, cut and fit, accessories, and color combinations are the kinds of thing you should be looking for and discussing with the designer. You will also want to have your actors go through any out-of-the-ordinary movements/blocking/choreography in a given costume, to make sure there is no constriction or danger of tearing.

Another benefit to the costume parade is that it allows stage managers to go through the script and take note of where all of the changes happen and look for problem spots. The designer will have given stage management a costume plot (Figure 11.1), indicating what each actor is wearing in a given scene.

Proof Costume Plot
Payton Wilburn, Costume Designer; Destiny Garcia, Costume Assistant

Hal:	Claire:
• 1.1 ○ Khaki slacks ○ Navy polo ○ Sperry topsiders ○ Brown belt • 1.2 ○ Add jacket to 1.1 • 1.3 ○ Switch to Rock n' Roll shirt • 1.4 ○ Same as 1.3 • 2.1 ○ Switch to navy sweater • 2.2 ○ Same as 1.3 • 2.3 ○ Add grey cardigan • 2.5 ○ Swap cardigan for jacket.	• 1.2 ○ Plum blazer ○ Dark grey slacks ○ Off-white blouse ○ Black heels • 1.4 ○ "Hangover" sweats ○ White tee shirt ○ Slippers • 2.2 ○ Same as 1.4 • 2.3 ○ Light grey slacks ○ Purple satin blouse ○ Black heels • 2.5 ○ Add Brown sweater ○ Switch to brown heels
Catherine:	**Robert:**
• 1.1 ○ Brown knit sweater ○ Jeans ○ Sneakers • 1.2 ○ Same plot as 1.1 • 1.3 ○ Plain black dress ○ Army surplus jacket ○ Plain black flats • 1.4 ○ Same plot from 1.1, but with khakis • 2.1 ○ Loose fitting khaki pants ○ Sneakers ○ Plain brown t-shirt ○ Baggy green button down • 2.2 ○ Same plot as 1.4 • 2.4 ○ Khakis ○ Brown shirt ○ Grey coat ○ Sneakers • 2.5 ○ Khakis ○ Green sweater ○ Sneakers	• 1.1 ○ Khaki pants ○ Tan sweater ○ Penny loafers ○ Plain white shirt • 2.1 ○ Switch to green pull over sweater ○ Bucket hat • 2.4 ○ Plain white t-shirt ○ Khakis

165

Louisiana Tech University Department of Theatre

Figure 11.1 Example of a costume plot from David Auburn's *Proof*. (Source: Costume Designer Payton Wilburn; Costume Assistant Destiny Garcia; and the Louisiana Tech University Department of Theatre.)

Figure 11.1 shows a costume plot for a production of *Proof* by David Auburn. Notice that the character of Claire goes from sweats, a T-shirt, and slippers in Act II, scene ii to slacks, a blouse, and heels in the next scene. During a costume parade, while you are focusing on how the costume appears on the actress, stage management will be checking the script to see how long the actress has to make the change. If the time between Claire's exit in one costume and entrance in another is brief, then they know that a quick change will be needed. The costume parade is when these decisions begin to be made.

The biggest benefit of having a costume parade (something that not all companies do) is that it gives the designer and costume staff the time to make changes … sometimes substantial ones. The costume parade typically occurs far enough out that the costumers are still able to adjust to fit the actor, director, and production needs. As always, you must remember that the costume designer is your *collaborator*, and communicate accordingly. Ask questions and carry on a conversation—one that should include the actor, to ensure that there aren't unseen problems with any of the costume pieces.

Dress Rehearsals

In Chapter 10, we noted that, while we're discussing periods of rehearsal linearly for the purpose of the book, they often overlap in actuality. Occasionally, you will have what many call "dress-techs" (or "tech-dresses"), where the actors begin to wear costumes during technical rehearsals. In this instance, your primary focus will still be on technical elements, with only minimal attention given to the costumes. As you move into full dress rehearsals, though, your focus shifts to what the costumes add to the performances. Looking at (and noting) costumes is usually not as difficult as doing so with lights and sound. As with sets and props, it is usually very obvious if there is a problem with a costume. Whether it's a missing button, a pair of pants that need to have the hem let down, or a hat that's too small for an actor's head, costume problems tend to jump off the stage. Even though the designer will be taking his or her own notes, you need to notice them as well. Having gone through technical rehearsals, there will be fewer stops and starts during the run, allowing you to focus on the way the actors are wearing the costumes and how they affect the actors' movement, business, and characterization.

Assuming that you and your design team have discussed long ago how the costumes reflect character and fit in with the concept of the show, you will be giving more technical (as opposed to concept or thematic) notes during dress rehearsals. While that may seem like a simple enough task, many young directors have difficulty verbalizing *why* they are giving a note. I was once mentoring a graduate directing student who was working on a production of Qui Nguyen's *Stained Glass Ugly*. While giving notes after a dress rehearsal, the director requested a different dress for the actress. The costume designer, as expected, asked why. The director responded with "Ummmmm … I don't know." Now, I understood why the direct or gave that note (and I suspect the costume designer did too): the dress wasn't falling right on the actress, and didn't present a flattering picture within the framework of her blocking—but the young director didn't have the experience or vocabulary to articulate that. Through a series of questions, I was able to lead the director to the verbalization of this reason, but it was not instinctive. It's a learned skill, and one you will develop with experience.

167

Figure 11.2 The actress in *Stained Glass Ugly*, in the final costume. (L–R: Tyler Landry and Ashley Larson. Costume design by Robyn Barrows. Photo courtesy of Mark D. Guinn and the Louisiana Tech University Department of Theatre.)

Final Dress

In an online list about directing, teacher and director, De Elizabeth comments on the cliché of a "bad dress rehearsal leading to a good opening night," which "is a superstition because we desperately want to believe it. Bad dress rehearsals are actually pretty terrifying."[6] Elizabeth could not be more correct. While the phrase seems to be a staple among actors, directors know that the final dress should actually be the best run through the show that you've had. Operating under "performance conditions," final dress allows you to see the show one last time before the audience comes in for opening night. By this point, you will (hopefully) have given all the major technical and costume notes, and you can now turn your focus fully back to the actors. In actuality, your focus most likely shifted back to the actors earlier in the dress rehearsal period, as costume notes rarely occupy your full attention.

When it comes to notes for your actors now, you should either be looking at very big things or very small things. The specific physical, vocal, and character work should have long been completed, which was part of setting the show as you moved into tech rehearsals. Here, then, you're looking at big, obvious things—pacing, stage business, entrances and exits, stage pictures, etc.—and small, detailed things—adjusting blocking by half a step to make sure an actor is in the light or instructing an actor to tilt a hat back a bit so his or her face isn't in shadow. Fight any urge you might have to re-direct the show, and understand that you are now at a point where the show pretty much is what it is. Wholesale changes at this point will only serve to confuse your actors and anger your production team. Your notes after final dress should be brief, positive, and encouraging, to actors and crew alike.

A final word on giving notes throughout techs and dresses. We've emphasized in this chapter the importance of articulating specific reasons when giving notes, but like any rule there will be exceptions. Directors will often give a note simply because it "feels" right. You may find yourself wanting to give a note and knowing it's the right one to give, without knowing why. Trusting your instinct and intuition about things is not necessarily a bad thing, but you really do need to have experience in learning *which* instincts and intuitions to trust (see the "dropping the baby from the grid" story in Chapter 3 for an example of when *not* to trust an instinct). The play *D'Arc Comedy*, by Wanda Strukus, is a comedic look at the life of Joan of

168

Arc, told through song, dance, TV chat shows, and puppets. One of the final scenes is a cartoonish depiction of Joan's burning at the stake, and I told the sound designer that I wanted Rupert Holmes' song "Escape" (also known as "The Pina Colada Song") to play as the flames rose around Joan. The designer, appropriately enough, questioned my motives for such a choice and was extremely hesitant to put it in. I had no idea why, but I just *knew* that the juxtaposition of that song with that moment was the perfect absurd touch the scene needed. I finally succeeded in talking the designer into trying it, and that scene wound up getting the biggest laugh of the show every night. Sometimes, you *do* simply "go with your gut." French director Louis Jouvet once said that the "director is indefinable because his functions are undefined."[7] That undefined quality can serve you well; it just takes experience to learn how.

Exercises and Suggested Reading

Exercise

1. Read Molière's *Tartuffe*, and then get into groups of three. Assign one person to be the director, the costume designer, and the actor. Assume that you are working on a production of the play with a concept set in modern-day Dallas, TX and Tartuffe is a televangelist. Using your department's costume stock and/or your own items, the costume designer and actor in your group should create a costume for one of the characters in the play (without input from the director). Hold a "costume parade," and after the director should give notes on what works and what doesn't with the costume. Class members should critique each director on the way he or she gives notes. Some things to consider:

   a. Did the director show a grasp of the costume designer's intent?

   b. Did the director identify what did and did not work with the costume?

   c. Did the director fully articulate the reasons for any requested changes?

   d. Did the director utilize a communication style that fostered collaboration (as opposed to a dictatorial style)?

Notes

1. Lawrence Stern, *Stage Management* (New York: Routledge, 2013 (1981)), 103.
2. W. Oren Parker, Harvey K. Smith, and R. Craig. Wolf, *Scene Design and Stage Lighting* (New York: Holt, Rinehart, and Winston, 1985 (1963)), 366.
3. Tom Markus and Linda Sarver, *Another Opening, Another Show: A Lively Introduction to the Theatre* (Boston: McGraw Hill, 2005 (2001)), 138.
4. Tennessee Williams, *A Streetcar Named Desire* (New York: Signet, 1947), 96.
5. Mary Fran Crook, text message to the author, November 14, 2015.
6. "Ten Things All Theatre Directors Know To Be True," Thought Catalog, last modified May 29, 2014, thoughtcatalog.com/de-elizabeth/2014/05/10-things-all-theatre-directors-know-to-be-true/.
7. Louis Jouvet, "The Profession of the Director," in Toby Cole and Helen Krich Chinoy (eds), *Directors on Directing: A Sourcebook of the Modern Theater* (Forest Grove, OR: Allegro Editions, 2013 (1963)), 227.

Suggested Reading

Auburn, David. *Proof* (New York: Dramatists Play Service, 2000).

Cole, Toby and Chinoy, Helen Krich (eds). *Directors on Directing* (Forest Grove, OR: Allegro Editions, 2013 (1963)).

Feldshuh, David. *Miss Evers' Boys* (New York: Dramatists Play Service, 1998 (1992)).

Inge, William. *Bus Stop* (New York: Dramatists Play Service, 1955).

Markus, Tom and Sarver, Linda. *Another Opening, Another Show* (New York: McGraw-Hill, 2004 (2001)).

Molière. *Tartuffe* (*c.*1664, available online).

Nguyen, Qui. *Stained Glass Ugly* (New York: Vampire Cowboys, 2003).

Stern, Lawrence. *Stage Management* (New York: Routledge, 2013 (1981)).

Strukus, Wanda. *D'Arc Comedy* (Chicago, IL: Dramatic Publishing, 2014).

PART V

OPENING NIGHT AND BEYOND

CHAPTER 12

It's Open ...
Now What?

Peter Brook, arguably the greatest director who has ever lived, once said of audiences: "In a sense, there is nothing a spectator can actually do. And yet there is a contradiction here that cannot be ignored, for everything depends on him."[1] Your play, ultimately, does depend on the audience to complete the production, for without the audience, everything is just an extended rehearsal. Jerzy Grotowski has said that, for "the average theatre-goer, the theatre is first and foremost a place of entertainment."[2] While Grotowski was making the point rather scornfully in the context of his book, he is, nevertheless, correct. As a director, you must remember that, while the theatre is your medium to tell stories and illuminate ideas, the audience is attending, hoping to find an enjoyable evening out. And ultimately, all of the decisions you've made in this process have been geared toward how the audience will respond.

Before we get to opening night, let's take a moment to discuss previews. As you advance in your career, you may find yourself working for a company that holds preview performances ahead of the actual opening. Previews can be an extraordinary tool for a director (and, if working with a new play, for the playwright), as they give you the opportunity to judge an audience's response to the show, while still having the chance to give notes and make changes. If you are able to hold preview performances, gauge how the audience responds and weigh that response against what your hopes and expectations were. You won't be making wholesale changes (unless you're working with a playwright and a new script that may undergo significant rewrites), but you are afforded the opportunity to make small tweaks to

173

guarantee that each moment of the show is succeeding in the manner you intended.

Once a show is open, the job of the director becomes somewhat nebulous. In the professional world, your contract typically ends with your final paycheck on opening night. In the case of shows with extended runs, you may be contracted to come back in for pick-up rehearsals or put-in rehearsals (rehearsing to put in understudies or replacement performers), but particularly early in your career, your job will be finished once the show is open. Navigating the path of praise and (because it's unavoidable) criticism is not always an easy thing. You can never let your emotions get too high or too low, but keeping an even keel isn't simple. In order to simplify all of this, I will divide this chapter into four loose sections ("loose" because, as always, there is some overlap): opening night, responding to audiences, responding to critics, and the post-mortem.

Opening Night

It is no secret that opening night is the most exciting element of any production for almost all involved. The weeks (sometimes months, sometimes years) of hard work are paying off with the opportunity to share your story with the audience. As the opening has drawn closer and closer, your role as cheerleader for the company has grown and grown, so that "By opening night the cast ought to be convinced that their interpretation of the play and their individual roles are the best they are capable of at this time."[3] Depending on the traditions or expectations of the theatre where you are working, you may have a big company meeting prior to opening, or you may just spend the time before curtain visiting with cast members as individuals or in small groups. Whatever the habits of the company, use the time to check in with your actors' emotional states. I know this is a bit touchy-feely-artsy-fartsy, but nerves and stage fright are universal, and affect even the most seasoned performers. You can certainly offer reminders about small points here and there, but don't try to give any big notes, or you will find that you have done nothing more than confuse your actor.

As curtain time approaches, you may very well be dealing with nerves of your own. Many young directors (and many experienced ones, for that matter) find that they are too nervous to watch the show with the audience on opening night, fearing that every laugh line might not hit, or that that one problem piece of stage business

174

might not work. While it's natural to worry, take the advice of Elsa the Snow Queen in *Frozen* and "let it go." The beauty of live theatre as an art form is that anything truly is possible. And the genius of actors is in their capacity to adapt and grow in a performance. Mistakes, surprises, and the unexpected are *going* to happen, so it's best if you work not to agonize over them.

Not agonizing over things is one thing, but no one is asking you to ignore them. You are, obviously, going to view the show with a different eye than the rest of the audience. You will notice every dropped line, late entrance, or misplaced cue. It is fine to take notes during opening night, but just as we discussed in Chapter 11 about final dress, you do not need to take major, character or performance-changing notes. Small gags, entrances, actors finding their light, pacing, etc.: those are the types of things you can (and should) note on opening night. The key thing to remember, however, is that *you* do not give the notes to the actors. Once you made it to techs and dresses, the show became the PSM's. The PSM is the person in charge and should be the one to give notes to the cast and company. Give your notes to the PSM to give to the actors, so that you can concentrate on congratulating them on their hard work and brilliant performances.

An exception to this often comes in educational and/or community theatres. With fewer performances, many directors in these companies will watch each performance and give notes each night. The thought process behind this is that it is a learning experience and the director can still take the opportunity to use each performance as a teaching moment (indeed, some directing books advocate this). I, however, am a proponent of treating each production as a professional one, and leaving the show alone after opening. The weeks of rehearsals and preparation have led to this moment, and the show now belongs to the PSM, the running crew, and the company. Allow them to experience, learn, and grow in their roles, with the play as the living, breathing organism that it is.

Another reason I advocate the "hands-off" approach is for the benefit of the actors. Every actor experiences an endorphin-adrenaline high on opening night. That excitement translates into motivation for them to continue to learn and grow in their roles, and nothing puts an immediate damper on it more than a barrage of notes that seemingly ignore all of their work but focus (as notes tend to do) on the negative. The way that I learned this first-hand, comes from an example that I use with my students all of the time, from my own grad school years. I was acting in a production of David Mamet's *Oleanna*, directed by another grad student, who is an outstanding director and a dear friend. After a wonderfully successful (or so I thought) opening night, my father came backstage and raved about the show. Not only that, he called me later on to rave about the show. This was significant. While my dad loved theatre and supported everything I did, he was not one to rave about a show; this was the first time that he had ever done so. As I walked into the theatre building the next morning, I met the director coming down the hall. As he knew my dad and would understand the significance of his excitement about the show, I recounted the post-show experience and subsequent phone call. The director's response? "Yeah. yeah. That's great. Now, I've got some notes." He then proceeded to sit me down and give three pages of notes on my opening night performance. It was, as you might expect, one of the biggest "downers" I've ever had in my career. Quietly I sat, absorbing the notes, and went on to complete the run somewhat joylessly.

Now, years later, the director and I talked about it at length and he understood what a horrible experience that was for me. We laugh about it now, because it was a learning experience for both of us (which is, of course, the point of graduate school), but it was pretty devastating at the time. In retrospect, however, I'm glad that it happened, because it was a valuable learning experience and has colored the way I have pursued my career, and shaped my hands-off opening night position. So, use this to your own advantage and allow your actors the chance to enjoy the entire experience of the production.

Responding to Audiences

With luck, responding to the opening night audience is a simple task of gracefully accepting congratulations and laudatory comments with a smile and a handshake. The opening night audience is typically the most excited to be there, filled with family and friends of the company, all of whom are more than willing to ignore or forgive that static from the mic or the moment the pen broke. They will swarm you and praise you and generally adore you, and your job is to smile and thank them and ask them to tell all of their friends about the show.

Occasionally, however, an audience member will be dissatisfied about some aspect of the show. Depending on where you are working, you may or may not come in contact with these unhappy folks. It may be that the house manager, box office supervisor, artistic director, marketing director, or some other staff member is the person to whom the disgruntled customer comes, but whether you are the recipient of the customer's displeasure or not, you should know how to deal with these people. The first rule to remember is that *they have a right to their opinion.* When faced with unhappy audience members, you cannot fall into the trap of scorning or belittling their opinion with an attitude, "Well, you're wrong and you just didn't get it." I once directed a production of Shakespeare's *Henry IV, Parts I and II* (an adaptation that combined both scripts into one evening). The concept was a postmodern one, and early in the show on opening night, a woman angrily stormed out of the theatre, walked into the booth, and began complaining to the PSM while she was calling the show! The PSM calmly alerted staff members who visited with the patron in the lobby to hear her grievance. Her complaint? That the show "wasn't really Shakespeare" because the actors weren't in Elizabethan dress!

It would have been easy for me (or any of the production team) to take the position that she just didn't "get" the concept of the show, but that would have been dismissive of her position and is *not* the way to interact with your patrons. Remember Grotowski's quote at the beginning of this chapter about why people come to the theatre. If audiences aren't happy with their experience, they have every right to voice their concerns. (We're assuming here that the hypothetical patron is expressing their displeasure in an appropriate manner, and not being disruptive or otherwise adversely affecting the rest of the audience and the company.)

No, when faced with the voiced displeasure of an audience, recall the old adage of retail workers everywhere, "the customer is always right." That doesn't mean that you alter your intent or purpose according to each patron's whim. What it *does* mean is that you listen to the audience's concerns, acknowledge their displeasure, and do what you can to placate them. Most audience members who complain simply want to be heard. A great phrase to use when faced with such complaints is "I'm sorry that you didn't enjoy your evening with us, but I do hope that you'll come back for one of our future shows. We produce a wide variety of work and we certainly hope that you'll find an offering that you enjoy." After that, unless you are the artistic director or are in some other management position for the company, you simply disengage from the patron. If your company has a refund policy or the ability to offer comps to a future show, then allow the appropriate staff member to handle that part of the transaction.

An important thing to remember is that *someone* will always be unhappy or offended by a play, no matter what it is. Do not allow those opinions to color your own feelings for the plays you direct. You cannot control or dictate taste, nor should you, as not everything is for everyone (or, as my dad always said, "That's why they have chocolate ice cream—not everyone likes vanilla"). You may feel that a show is the most family-friendly one around, but someone, somewhere will find a reason to take offense. During my first year teaching at a small, privately owned Methodist college, I chose a season that was (in my mind) the most wholesome, fun, family-friendly one possible. The first play of the year was Beth Henley's *The Miss Firecracker Contest*: a sweet, Southern comedy that our small-town, Southern audiences were sure to love. The day after a wildly successful opening night, a professor from the business department came into my office to tell me how mortified he was by the show—so much so that he, his wife, and their guests had to get up and leave the theatre (which I had not noticed). When I asked what had sparked his outrage, he said he was *scandalized* that an actress appeared onstage in a bathing suit! If you're not familiar with Henley's script, it centers around a small-town beauty pageant, in which characters naturally appear onstage in swimsuits. Now, the bathing suit in question was, by most standards, a pretty modest one: a one-piece suit that was neither low cut nor cut high on the legs. While I (and most everyone else) saw nothing of concern with this costume, the professor, who was older and obviously subscribed to different standards, did. And that's OK. I thanked him for coming to me with his thoughts, apologized for his less-than-stellar experience, and invited him to the next production (the musical comedy *Snoopy*). We became great friends, and he and his wife were wonderful supporters of our small theatre program, but he always "screened" each production by asking me about it ahead of time. Had I not taken the time to listen to his concerns and engage him in conversation, I (and our department) would have lost out on the support and friendship of a great patron. Take my advice: *listening* is one of the best attributes you can have.

Responding to Critics

Oscar Wilde, a notable hater of critics, once said, "The critic has to educate the public; the artist has to educate the critic."[4] In pursuit of this, Wilde was known to write scathing letters to the editors of newspapers that published criticisms of his work. While I may not subscribe to the hubris of the second half of Wilde's statement, the first half is absolutely correct. As an artist, understand that the theatre critic serves a vital function in the production process, becoming a type of "advance scout" for the general public. The true professional critic will have researched and studied the play, playwright, and company ahead of time. He or she will have an idea of the goals of the production and will evaluate the performance accordingly, offering the public an idea of what they can expect when they come to the theatre.

On Broadway and the West End, there is an unwritten agreement between producers and critics that writers will not publish reviews before the established opening date. Unfortunately, this is sometimes broken, as was the case when *The Times* published an unflattering review from a 2015 preview performance of the Barbican's *Hamlet*, starring Benedict Cumberbatch. The resultant public relations firestorm drove interest in the production, already at fever pitch due to Cumberbatch's worldwide celebrity, even higher … which, most likely, was the opposite from the critic's intent. Incidents like this are, thankfully, isolated, and in cities and towns much smaller than New York and London it typically isn't a problem at all, since local critics and media outlets usually have an established relationship and protocol with local arts organizations.

Wherever you are, when you read, watch, or listen to reviews of your production, keep in mind the old theatre saying that "you're never as good as they say and you're never as bad as they say." Like the audience members discussed in the previous section, everyone is entitled to their own opinions. We certainly hope that a professional critic will have a better researched and more insightful opinion (that is, after all, the critic's job), but it is still a subjective process. How does one quantify an ethereal art form like theatre? One of the best ways to learn how theatre criticism works is to become a critic in your own right. On the website, you will find the performance critique sheet. By completing this worksheet, and either leaving your answers in bulleted form or using your answers to craft an essay-style

Performance Critique Sheet

Use the following criteria as a method of performance evaluation. Your final critique can either be listed in this format, or you may use your answers to craft an essay-style critique. Use the blanks on the right to evaluate each topic of consideration for a performance.

1. Blocking	
A. Movement	
B. Integration	
C. Business	
D. Pictures	
2. Characterization	
A. Physical	
B. Vocal	
C. Intention	
D. Commitment	
3. Story	
A. Clarity	
B. Intent	
C. Arc	
D. Completeness	
4. Concept	
A. Source	
B. Purpose	
C. Cohesiveness	
D. Execution	
5. Direction	
A. Grasp	
B. Ensemble	
C. Design	
D. Overall	

Figure 12.1 Performance critique sheet.

review, you will develop a critical eye for the work of directors that will inevitably improve your own work in the field.

Think of each section of the performance critique sheet as a series of questions you can ask and, by answering them, establish a critical perspective on a director's work. Make sure that when you answer the questions you are also considering the unspoken "why?" for each one.

1. *Blocking.* In this section, you are scrutinizing and critiquing how the director has used the actors in the space provided by the architecture of the theatre and the scenic design for the show.
   a. *Movement.* How well did the director move the actors around the space? Does the flow of movement seem organic and natural, or forced and mechanical?
   b. *Integration.* Does the director's blocking work *with* the scenic design or *against* it? Does the director use the entire design? Are all available acting areas used in a natural and logical fashion?
   c. *Business.* Do the gestures and stage business performed by the actors make sense within the world of the play? Are properties and items used in a natural and logical fashion?
   d. *Pictures.* Did the director develop any "snapshot moment" stage pictures? What were the most effective stage pictures in the show?
2. *Characterization.* In this section you are critiquing the performance of the actors and, by extension, the direction they have been given. You should complete this section for all principal characters in the show.
   a. *Physical.* Did the actors use any physical adjustments or characterization in their development of the role? Did the physical characteristics of the actors fit with both the character and the style of the show?
   b. *Vocal.* Did the actors use any vocal adjustments or characterization in their development of the role? Did the vocal characteristics of the actors fit with both the character and the style of the show?
   c. *Intention.* Were the character's intentions clear? Could you see that the actor (character) was pursuing an objective and dealing with obstacles in a manner consistent with the show?

181

      d. *Commitment.* Were the actors committed to their roles (and thus, the show)? Did the actors support the performances of their castmates?

3. *Story.* In this section, you are considering and critiquing the story being told by the play, and how effectively the director and company told that story.

      a. *Clarity.* Was the story of the play told with clarity? Were you able to tell whose story it is?

      b. *Intent.* What do you surmise was the director's intent in telling the story? Does the director's intent seem to mesh with the playwright's, or are they working at cross-purposes?

      c. *Arc.* Did the performance have an arc to it? Was there a building of action and story that drew you in and led you to the end of the play? Was the story of the play told at an effective pace and rhythm?

      d. *Completeness.* Did the play's performance have a finished feel? Was there a completeness to the story being told that allowed you, as an audience member, to view it holistically?*

4. *Concept.* In this section, you are critiquing the directorial concept of the production. Remember, there's no such thing as a production without a concept: "traditional" is a concept in and of itself.

      a. *Source.* Does the concept used by the director tie in to the source material (the script)? Does it make sense to use this concept, or does it feel "forced" onto the play?

      b. *Purpose.* What do you judge the director's purpose to be for using this concept? What did the director hope to achieve or illuminate by using the concept? Was the director successful in this?

      c. *Cohesiveness.* Is the concept carried through the entire production? Do all design elements, as well as performances, adhere to the concept? Is the concept carried over to the entire theatre-going experience (lobby decor, program style, etc.)?

      d. *Execution.* Was the concept well executed? Did it work?

---

* Bear in mind that some plays are open-ended or do not have a satisfactory resolution. That is not what this question is asking you to consider.

5. *Direction*. In this section, you are evaluating the overall work of the director and critiquing the performance as a whole.
   a. *Grasp*. Did the director have a firm grasp on the playwright's intent and effectively create a production that brought the characters and situations to life?
   b. *Ensemble*. Did the cast work together well as an ensemble? Did they all seem to be "living in the same world?" Were there any cast members who stood out (either positively or negatively)?
   c. *Design*. Did the director make effective use of all of the design elements in the production? Was the director able to work seamlessly with the design elements in a way that supported the actors and the story?
   d. *Overall*. What is your overall summation of the production? Are there elements that stuck out to you that have not been covered elsewhere in the critique?

Post-Mortem

In their book *The Director's Vision*, Louis Catron and Scott Shattuck quote Peter Brook:

When a performance is over, what remains? ... It is the play's central image that remains, its silhouette, and if the elements are rightly blended this silhouette will be its meaning, this shape will be the essence of what it has to say.[5]

Brook's quote, from *The Empty Space*, showcases exactly why a director should always perform a post-mortem after a production. The post-mortem is an opportunity for you to evaluate the production honestly and consider how well you accomplished what you had hoped. On the website you will find a post-mortem worksheet that will allow you to organize your thoughts and your own self-critique of the production. While you may choose to conduct a more informal, verbal post-mortem with a professor or colleague, the worksheet will provide you with a template of matters for your consideration. In order for this process to be effective, you have to be completely and utterly honest with yourself. That means you cannot give in either to blind celebration or to despairing criticism. Address each section with a clear and open assessment of your work.

You will notice that the columns for each section are the same: "goals," "success," and "reasons." In each part, you should consider

Post-mortem Worksheet

Director Name: **Show Title:**

Theatre Name: **Performance Dates:**

Script

Goal(s)	Success	Reason(s)

Cast

Goal(s)	Success	Reason(s)

Concept

Goal(s)	Success	Reason(s)

Design

Goal(s)	Success	Reason(s)

Figure 12.2 The post-mortem worksheet.

Goal(s)	Success	Reason(s)

Overall

Goal(s)	Success	Reason(s)

Figure 12.2 Continued.

what it is you were trying to accomplish, how successful (or not) you were in that goal, and why things might have worked (or not). The purpose behind this is for you to be able to build on your successes, and develop an awareness of what has not worked, and why, in an effort to improve the next time you direct. Ultimately, this will allow you to grow and develop as a theatre artist. Let's briefly look at each section.

Script
Why did you choose this script to direct? What story were you hoping to tell? What themes were you trying to illuminate? What did you want the audience to take away after seeing the performance?

Cast
Go back and look at your casting and audition notes (Chapter 5). What type of cast were you looking for? Why did you choose the actors you did? How successful were you in working with your cast, and how successful were they in bringing the characters to life onstage?

Concept

What concept did you use with the production? Why? Was it successful and did it accomplish what you'd hoped? If you were to direct the show again, would you choose a similar concept or a different one?

Design

How satisfied were you with the experience of working with the show's designers? How well did the design work with your concept and with the show as a whole? Were all the special needs of the show met with the design elements?

Performances

How satisfied were you with your experience of working with the cast? How well did you feel you communicated with the actors? How successful were you in directing them to achieve the performances that you wanted?

Overall

How satisfied were you with the production as a whole? What was your experience working with the company members and theatre administration? Is this a company for whom you would like to work again?

Remember the key to all of this is your honesty with the evaluation, which is the only way that it can be beneficial for you.

What's Next?

Congratulations! You have successfully directed and opened a show, and are ready to move on to the next one. While directors are not nearly as nomadic as actors, there is a bit of movement for them. Another reason that most directors' contracts end with opening night is that they are by then moving on to the next gig. At the very least, most directors are beginning to work on or think about the next gig as opening night for the current one rolls around. But how do you *get* the next gig? The final chapter of the book will provide you with the tools for putting together a directing portfolio to use as you pursue the next step in your professional career.

Exercises and Suggested Reading

Exercises

1. Attend a production (either one of your department's or one at a different theatre) as a class. Critique the show using the performance critique sheet found on the website and explained in this chapter. Share your thoughts with your classmates to see what they might have noticed that you did not.
2. Use one of the ten-minute-play scripts found in the Appendix (or another of your choosing) as a directing project. If time allows, go through the entire process of direction, from research to performance. Then utilize the post-mortem worksheet to evaluate your work on the show. *Note:* I understand that the constraints of your class may not allow for this, but you may be able to modify it to fit your own particular needs.

Notes

1. Peter Brook, *The Empty Space* (New York: Touchstone, 1968), 21.
2. Jerzy Grotowski, *Towards a Poor Theatre* (New York: Routledge, 2002), 28.
3. John W. Kirk and Ralph A. Bellas, *The Art of Directing* (Belmont, CA: Wadsworth, Inc., 1985), 188.
4. Oscar Wilde, *Letters on Dorian Gray* (VIII, originally written to the *Scots Observer*, August 16, 1890), accessed November 14, 2015, www.readbookonline.net/readOnLine/9894/.
5. Louis E. Catron and Scott Shattuck, *The Director's Vision, Play Direction from Analysis to Production* (Long Grove, IL: Waveland Press, Inc., 2016), 15.

Suggested Reading

Brook, Peter. *The Empty Space* (New York: Touchstone, 1995 (1968)).

Brook, Peter. *The Shifting Point* (New York: Theatre Communications Group, 1994 (1987)).

Shakespeare, William. *Henry IV, Part II* (c.1596–1599, available online).

Wilde, Oscar. *The Picture of Dorian Gray*, adapted by John Osborne (New York: Samuel French, 2011 (1973)).

CHAPTER 13

The Director's Portfolio

Actors have auditions. Designers have portfolios full of beautiful sketches, renderings, and photographs. Stage managers have prompt books and reams of paperwork. All of those items are used to pursue future jobs, but what about directors? Outside of a résumé and an interview, what do directors have to show that they are qualified to be hired? The title of this chapter, of course, has given the answer to that question away: the *director's portfolio*.

Portfolios for directors are a somewhat nebulous thing, as there are no established criteria for what constitutes a "standard" directing portfolio. Part of the reason is that many companies hire directors based on recommendations, word of mouth, or familiarity (a director has worked for a company in another capacity, and the company then hires him or her to direct). Because there is nothing that is truly considered industry-standard, what you will find in this chapter is a basic template for what to include in your portfolio. Portfolios can be either electronic or hard copy (and we will discuss both options later in the chapter), but the key to any format is that it is well organized, clean, and easy to follow.

Before getting to a discussion of electronic versus hard-copy formats, let's examine what you should have in your portfolio. You will adapt your portfolio based on the job for which you are interviewing, including show-specific information, but there are certain elements you will always want to include: a director's statement, your résumé, production photographs, and video. We'll discuss each of these individually, but before we do, a word of caution: before including any production photographs or performance video samples of your work in your portfolio, make certain that you have received permission from the appropriate companies to do so. Obtaining permissions and giving proper credit is actually part of your portfolio, in that it shows potential employers that you are conscious of the idea of artistic ownership and aware of copyright. Notice that, throughout this book, any time I have included a production photograph as an example I have credited both the photographer and the theatre company, since each photo is a representation of their work. Now, on to the portfolio elements.

Director's Statement

If you go to an art gallery or showing, it is common to see an artist's statement displayed, either on the wall or in the show's program or guidebook. Visual artists (including theatrical designers) are taught to develop an artistic statement that expresses their aesthetic and vision as they put together a show. For directors, this is typically covered by the concept statement you develop for a show, but for your portfolio you should think in terms of an overall vision. Your director's statement is something that you will develop over time, and it will most likely change and grow as you do. Think of your director's statement as an expression of your philosophy of directing. Someone reading it should be able to get a feel for how and why you direct, and how you generally approach working on a project. Though you will eventually present your statement in a paragraph, to go about developing it, ask yourself the following questions:

189

Why do I direct? Answer this question in the "macro" sense. Don't think about it in terms of "why do I want to direct a given show?" (that will come later)—but rather "why do I want to be a director?" Think of this question from the perspective of why you choose to be a director, as opposed to some other kind of artist. What is it that draws you to directing as an art form? Is it the storytelling? The overall vision? The research? The collaboration? Finding the answer to this question is more difficult than you might think, and requires you to engage in a bit of honest introspection. Most of the time, no matter the profession, we get caught up in everything we have to do for a given project and the details that make up our to-do list, and we don't stop to consider why it is we do what we do. The answer to this question is different for every director, because it is so personal. Tony Award-winning director Lloyd Richards has often related a story about meeting a cleaning woman in line to buy a ticket to a performance of his production of *A Raisin in the Sun* in Philadelphia. Meeting the woman had a rather profound impact on him, prompting him to say:

Now, that's why I'm in the theater. To take those lives, to reveal them. Not just those lives, any life. And that's what's important about theater, or should be. It does reflect the lives of a totality of a community that exists out there, and does speak to the totality of that community.[1]

Take the time to think about what it is about directing that draws you to the profession. Discuss it with your classmates and see how different (or similar) everyone's reasons are.

What inspires me? Some directors are inspired by the work of other directors. Some are inspired by artists in different media or specific artworks. Some draw inspiration from certain cultures or activities. As with the previous question, this isn't asking what inspires you for a specific production, but what inspires you overall, as an artist. Bijan Sheibani, Associate Director of the National Theatre of Great Britain, notes that he was inspired early on by seeing the work of the Obie Award-winning English director Katie Mitchell. "The emotional impact was so strong and frightening. I didn't know until then that theatre could have anything as like [the] impact [of] film."[2] The impact Sheibani discovered in Mitchell's direction served as inspiration to him for his own career. Remember, though, that your inspiration needn't come specifically from theatre artists. You may find that a particular style of music or the work of a certain painter or writer inspires you creatively and artistically. It might not even be an artist at all: perhaps you have a favorite location—a path in the woods, a river bank, a rooftop—that gets your creative juices flowing. That's what you're looking for in answering this question: what is it that engages your creativity and serves as a wellspring when you need to replenish it?

What do I hope to accomplish? This question isn't about career goals, but creative ones. What do you want to do with your work and what do you hope people will take away from it? That's what you are attempting to answer here. As a creative artist, what is it that you want audiences to experience when they watch your shows? It may be that you want to provoke audiences into discussion and consideration of serious topics, leading you to productions of shows such as *Keely and Du* or *The Suit*. Maybe you would like audiences to consider the intricacies of relationships between families and those as close as families, which prompts you to take on scripts like *August: Osage County* and *Becket or the Honour of God*. Perhaps your primary goal is to produce fun evenings of entertainment for all audiences, and so you take on projects like *Charlie and the Chocolate Factory* and *Oklahoma!* Many directors find that answering the question of what they want to accomplish leads them to a particular style or genre, though it doesn't have to be like that. There are, of course, some directors who are equally adept in any form, and enjoy using all of them. Sir Trevor Nunn, who brought *Cats*, *Les Misérables*, and *Nicholas Nickleby* (among many, many others) to the stage has said that he has "never had any feeling of disconnection between the classical theater, or the contemporary theater, or musical theater, or that thing we call opera."[3] Because of this approach, of course, he became one of the greatest directors the stage has seen. What will your approach be, and what will it lead *you* to accomplish?

Once you have answered these questions, put your thoughts together into a brief paragraph. Remember, this isn't an essay or an academic treatise. Whether on a website or in a binder, your director's statement is meant to be read rather quickly and should give the reader a thumbnail insight into and solid idea about your artistic aesthetic, before viewing the rest of your portfolio.

191

Résumé

As with so much of what we do, there are as many ways to format a résumé as there are people to tell you how. Most word-processing programs allow you to include designs and watermarks that let you personalize your résumé and help establish yourself as a kind of "brand," with your own logo and representation of your artistic aesthetic. Additionally, there are numerous websites that provide templates and ideas for résumé layout and formatting. It is acceptable to use any of these, as long as your résumé includes these five items:

1. *Your name.* This should be the first thing to draw our attention. A colleague with whom I once worked suggested taping your résumé on the wall, walking away ten steps, and then turning around. If your name isn't the first thing you can (easily) see, then it should be in a larger font.
2. *Your contact information.* Email addresses, phone numbers, answering services, etc. are all great things to have on your

résumé. You want people to be able to contact you easily, though, so make sure any contact source you put on your résumé is one that you check regularly. If you have representation, you put your agent's name and contact info on your résumé. One thing to remember … *never* put your address on your résumé. While it's unfortunate that we have to think this way, there are too many unsavory characters out there, and you do not want to advertise your location.

3. *Your experience.* Just as we tell actors: the older you get, and the more experience you get, you will begin to drop shows from your résumé. At this point in your career, when you probably do not have many directing credits, there will be other items that you include on your directing résumé (we will get to those in a minute) that show your leadership skills and abilities. There are a variety of ways you can organize your experience on the page, and we'll look at some examples below.

4. *Your training.* This can either be *where* you trained (Northeastern Oklahoma Technical Military College) or *with whom* you trained (world-famous directors Sally Smith and Joe Jones). This is another item that will eventually drop off of your résumé as you move further into your career. At some point, you will have worked enough that people are much more concerned about your experience than your training, and you won't need this section on your résumé.

5. *Your memberships* (if applicable). Are you a member of the SDC (Stage Directors and Choreographers Society) or some other union? Then have that on your résumé. Do you belong to any professional theatre organizations, like AEA (Actors Equity Association), ATHE (Association for Theatre in Higher Education), SETC (Southeastern Theatre Conference), or VASTA (Voice and Speech Trainers Association)? Then you should include those as well.

As long as your résumé includes those items, in a clean, easy-to-read format, you will be fine. The format, of course, is up to you. To give you an idea of possible formats, look at the following three methods of résumé organization.

Figure 13.1 shows an example of a résumé for a director who works across the country: in New York, at regional theatres, and at various colleges and universities. Notice that he has a wordmark "logo" based on his initials at the top of the page, with all of his

John Q. Director
SDC, ATHE

JQD@emailaddress.com   555.555.5555

New York Theatre

Night of the Iguana	Director	Primary Stages
Lysistrata	Director	Lucille Lortel Theatre
Three Tall Women	Director	Lucille Lortel Theatre
American Buffalo	Director	Second Stage Theatre
Sure Thing	Director	Expanded Arts, Inc.

Regional Theatre

Miss Evers' Boys	Director	The Alley Theatre
Parade	Director	Beef and Boards
Othello	Director	The Old Globe
Oklahoma!	Assistant Director	Goodman Theatre
The Music Man	Assistant Director	Goodman Theatre
1776	Assistant Director	The Guthrie Theatre

Educational Theatre

Romeo and Juliet	Director	University of Alabama
Arcadia	Director	University of Missouri
Two Gentlemen of Verona	Director	Columbia University
Of Mice and Men	Director	Louisiana Tech University

Education

University of Alabama	MFA, Directing	2001
Louisiana Tech University	BA, Theatre	1992

REFERENCES AVAILABLE UPON REQUEST

Figure 13.1 An example of a nationally based résumé.

contact and professional information. His experience is organized in a manner that allows the reader to see quickly where he has worked and on what shows, and he has structured it with his most impressive credits (in NYC) first.

Figure 13.2 shows a résumé for a director who has organized her experience based on different styles of shows. You will see that she has made a watermark logo for her page, and has formatted her contact information a little differently than the first example, but it

Sheila Director

Email: SheilaEDirector@email.com
Mobile: 111.111.1111

Musical Theatre

Into The Woods	Arkansas Rep
Disney's Beauty and the Beast	Theatre Four
Company	Spark State Theatre
Smoke on the Mountain	Ozarks Rep
Carousel	The Muny
Man of La Mancha	Gordo Shakespeare
Sweet Charity	University of Idaho

Classical Theatre

Macbeth	Alliance Theatre
Medea	Ohio Shakespeare
Henry V	The State Theatre
The Cherry Orchard	Andrew College
Timon of Athens	Post Playhouse
King Lear	Chicago Stages

Contemporary Theatre

The Little Dog Laughed	Topeka Playhouse
Fences	Arkansas Rep
The Last Night of Ballyhoo	Arkansas Rep
Picnic	Spark State Theatre
The Grapes of Wrath	Andrew College
Oleanna	The State Theatre
Hot l Baltimore	Iowa Onstage
The Miss Firecracker Contest	University of Idaho

References Available on Request

Figure 13.2 An example of a résumé organized by genre.

is still easy to read. Also, she has chosen not to include training, feeling that her experience is enough to get her a job. One of the biggest benefits of structuring your résumé like this is that it is easily customizable for any job application. You can swap sections around to feature the style of show you are seeking to direct: musical, classical, or contemporary.

Figure 13.3 is the style that will probably be most applicable to you at this stage of your career. You see that she only has two sections, one for theatrical experience and one she has called "related" experience. When you don't have a lot of directing credits to your name, you should include work that you have done that demonstrates you have some of the skills an employer might seek in a dir-

Millicent Fleming Director

MillicentFlemingDirector@email.com   *222.222.2222*

Theatrical Experience

The Illusion	Director	Louisiana Tech University
Christmas in July	Director	Trinity Presbyterian Church
Robin Hood	Assistant Director	Louisiana Tech University
Dearly Departed	Assistant Director	Louisiana Tech University
Dancing at Lughnasa	Assistant Director	Louisiana Tech University
A Man for All Seasons	Production Stage Manager	Town and Gown Players
A Christmas Carol	Production Stage Manager	Town and Gown Players
The Sound of Music	Assistant Stage Manager	Town and Gown Players
A Little Night Music	Assistant Stage Manager	Iowa State University
The Lion in Winter	Production Assistant	Iowa State University
Private Lives	Production Assistant	Iowa State University

Related Experience

Department of Theatre Office Manager	Louisiana Tech University
Summer Arts Camp Drama Instructor	Trinity Presbyterian Church
Drama Coordinator	Bryant Elementary School
After School Drama Teaching Assistant	Town and Gown Players
Shift Supervisor	Francenia's Boutique
Front Desk Worker	George's Clothier
Shop Assistant	Ellis Toy Company

Affiliations and Memberships

Southeastern Theatre Conference
Society of American Fight Directors

Education

Louisiana Tech University	Master of Arts in Theatre	2015
Iowa State University	Bachelor of Arts in Theatre	2012

References Available Upon Request

Figure 13.3 An example of a résumé for an early-career director.

ector, such as leadership, organization, dependability, etc. With that in mind, she has included assistant directing and stage management credits in her theatre section, and other work experience that indicates trustworthiness and responsibility in her "related" section.

As mentioned above, whichever format you choose for your résumé, of primary importance is that those reading it know exactly what they are looking at and don't have to try and figure it out. They want to be quickly able to see what kind of experience you've had and then move on to the rest of your portfolio.

Production Photographs

As previously mentioned, one key for using production photos is to make certain that you have the permission of the theatre company (and, by extension, the photographer) to use pictures from the show. Theatres will almost always grant you permission, but it's important to ask. When you do use the photos, make sure to credit the company and the photographer, at the very least. It's also good, where possible, to credit the designers and actors. Just as you want people to credit you for your work, you should show respect for their work by crediting them. The format in which you caption your photographs will depend on how you lay them out. If you have several photos from the same production set up on a page, you can do a single caption for the entire page. If you are displaying photos from a variety of shows, then you will need to caption each one individually. As with most of what we have discussed in the book, there is no single "right" way to display your production shots; the key is to make sure that they are laid out with an artistic eye and are aesthetically pleasing.

Choosing which photos to use says a lot about you as a director. Since they are still pictures, you will want to look for those "snapshot moments" we've discussed previously. Find shots that highlight your blocking and picturization: ones that feature a variety of levels and offer depth, as well as an interesting moment. One of the best things that can result from potential employers viewing your portfolio is that they ask, "What's going on in this picture?" That means you've captured their attention and now you have a chance to talk about your process. Additionally, select photographs that show the work of the designers in the best possible way.

Look at Figure 13.4, a photograph from *The Adventures of Robin Hood*. Notice that the photo is shot from an interesting angle, featuring the varying levels of height and depth between Robin and the Sheriff. You also get a sense of the design aesthetic for the sets and lighting, while the costume design features prominently. An excellent snapshot moment, this photograph captures the essence of the fun, swashbuckling show from which it comes.

Figure 13.4 The Adventures of Robin Hood with Robin (Jake Guinn) and the Sheriff (Matthew Ferguson). (Scenic Design: Holly Bricker; Costume Design: Sara Murdock; Lighting Design: Ryan Ferrebee. Photo courtesy of Mark D. Guinn, and the Louisiana Tech University Department of Theatre.)

Video

As with production photos, permission and credit is essential for the use of video. While you may think that you can only use video if you are creating an electronic portfolio, you can include it with a hard-copy presentation, though you will need to have it burned onto a disc or saved on a flash drive. There are two major considerations in selecting video clips: the quality of the video and its content.

Every theatre has its own method of archiving video footage, some more advanced than others. If you only have access to shaky, dark, or low-res video, it's probably best not to use it at all. Assuming you do have access to quality video, then you want to select footage that highlights your work as a director. Find scenes that showcase your movement of actors through space and utilization of the scenic and property elements, and use clips that come from climactic moments in the script to show how you handle them. Remember that the goal of providing video is to give artistic directors and producers an idea of what kind of production you put onstage as a director.

Show-Specific Elements

As we said above, you will adapt your portfolio with show-specific elements when necessary. If you are interviewing for a directing gig for a particular show, you want to show the person doing the hiring that you have given some thought to the production. While you usually wouldn't be expected to have a complete script analysis of the play, you can (and should) include an abbreviated one. In Chapter 4 we covered script analysis, and provided a worksheet on the website to use for it. For your portfolio, deal with sections I (structure) and III (character) of the script analysis. By working through these two sections you will have a foundational grasp of the show, and be able to discuss it in an interview. Additionally, completing these sections will allow you to begin formulating an idea for a concept, which you will want to outline briefly in a paragraph. By presenting this abbreviated analysis and concept, you will find yourself conversant enough with the show to engage in an excellent discussion with artistic directors or producers.

Formatting

Once you have gathered all the elements for your portfolio, you can then begin assembling them. Whether you choose to display your portfolio electronically or in hard-copy form is strictly up to you, although you may choose to have both formats ready and available. Regardless, just as with your résumé, the structure and organization should be clean and easy to read. If you put your portfolio into a physical binder, make sure that you include a table of contents and have each section tabbed and labeled, so someone looking at it can easily flip to any given section. If you put your portfolio together online, choose a hosting service that allows you to include an easily navigable menu tab, which, again, allows the person looking through it to quickly find specific material and jump to it. Remember that, like your résumé, a portfolio should present the same idea of yourself as a "brand." Find a cohesive look, style, or logo that appears throughout the portfolio and becomes easily identifiable as *you*.

In an online format, in addition to the contact information on your résumé, have a contact page that includes all the information. Many hosting services provide email forms that can be embedded on the page, and these are great. Links to your social media accounts (Twitter, Facebook, Instagram, etc.) can be included as long as your accounts are "professional" ones. Trust me, potential employers don't want to see pictures of you doing shots in Cabo during spring break! Another benefit to an electronic portfolio is the ability to link your photos and videos to the company where they were produced. Doing this allows viewers to get a more comprehensive look at your work if they desire, and helps out companies where you've worked by driving traffic to their sites.

As I said above, you might find that you want to create both electronic *and* hard-copy formats for your portfolio. Having an online presence that is, essentially, perpetual, is great for a director. You can include the URL on your résumé and business cards, and any correspondence you have with companies. As long as you update it regularly, it can be an ongoing part of your professional life. Once you have your site completed, when you go to an interview you have the option of bringing along a tablet or laptop to display it to potential employers. If, however, you find yourself in a location without internet access, then it's best to have your portfolio loaded on a disc, flash drive or tablet, or to have an excerpted hard copy. Should you choose the latter option, include your director's statement, résumé, and just a few photographs, with your website URL clearly marked on each page.

With your portfolio complete, you are set to sell yourself as a director. And make no mistake, this is just as important for directors as it is for actors going to audition. You want to engage potential employers, capture their attention, and make hiring you the most attractive option they have!

Exercises and Suggested Reading

Exercises

1. Answer the questions provided in the chapter and develop your director's artistic statement. Share it and compare it with the class.
2. Use one of the formats provided and create your résumé.
3. Use an online hosting service to create an electronic portfolio. Take elements from your website and create an abbreviated hard copy of your portfolio, as described in the chapter.

Notes

1. Academy of Achievement, "Lloyd Richards Interview—Academy of Achievement," last modified March 26, 2009, accessed December 24, 2015, www.achievement.org/autodoc/page/ric0int-2.
2. Anna Tims, "The Artists's Artist: Theatre Directors," *The Guardian*, November 9, 2011, accessed December 24, 2015, www.theguardian.com/culture/2011/nov/09/artists-artist-theatre-directors.
3. Academy of Achievement, "Sir Trevor Nunn Interview—Academy of Achievement," last modified July 15, 2015, accessed December 24, 2015, www.achievement.org/autodoc/page/nun0int-5.

Suggested Reading

Anouilh, Jean. *Becket or the Honour of God* (New York: Samuel French, 1959).

Edgar, David. *Nicholas Nickleby* (New York: Dramatists Play Service, 1982 (1980)).

Greig, David. *Charlie and the Chocolate Factory*. Currently available as Original Cast Recording (London: Sony, 2013).

Hammerstein II, Oscar (book and lyrics) and Rodgers, Richard (music). *Oklahoma!* (New York: Rodgers and Hammerstein Library, 1943).

Hansberry, Lorraine. *A Raisin in the Sun* (New York: Samuel French, 1959).

Krawczyk, Franck, Estienne, Marie-Hélène, and Brook, Peter. *The Suit* (Paris: Théâtre des Bouffes du Nord, 2013).

Letts, Tracy. *August: Osage County* (New York: Dramatists Play Service, 2007).

Martin, Jane. *Keely and Du* (New York: Samuel French, 2012 (1993)).

201

SCRIPTS FOR CLASS EXERCISES/ PRODUCTION

Appendix A

In this appendix and the following, you will find two ten-minute play scripts for use in class projects. Feel free to use them for the various exercises in the chapters, or for a class project or student-directed work. If directed and performed as part of a class assignment, there is no royalty fee assigned. If you would like to perform either piece outside of class as part of a public performance, please contact me with a request for rights.

LAVALOOOOO!!!

Paul B. Crook
Revised, 2006

Lavalooooo!!!

Characters

Floree   A determined woman of indeterminate age
Preston   A hyperactive man of 40
White-Coated   A white-coated attendant
  Attendant

Setting

The action takes place in a small room. It could be a waiting room. It could be an activity room. It could be a dining room. There is one table in the center of the room, surrounded by straight-backed chairs. Stage left is a long, narrow table, which could hold drinks, pamphlets, or any number of things. At the moment it holds a CD/radio/tape player. A worn-looking ottoman is against the wall stage right. Upstage right is a door. It is a normal-looking door, as doors go; however, we don't know where it leads ... or from whence it comes.

    It is the present.
    It is daytime.
    It is autumn.
    It is the South.

Lights up on Preston arranging flowers in a vase on the table. He is never able to get them quite to his liking. Adding to his difficulty is the fact that he is listening to a college football game on the radio … and living every play with the announcer's description of events. (Note: a tape of any recent college football game will do. Just make sure to pick an exciting segment.)

PRESTON. C'mon, c'mon. Hold 'em, dammit!
  (Note: This line and those following can be amended to fit the action you choose to use. "Score, dammit!" etc.) Awwwwwww, shit. The lilac can't go there. It ruins the line. Oh, for the love of—This is gonna kill me. *(Indicating flowers and radio)* One of these is going to kill me!
(Floree enters through the door.)
FLOREE. What's going to kill you? Or perhaps you're thinking of doing it yourself?
PRESTON. Oh it's just the game and these damn flowers. They—who the hell are you?
FLOREE. Me? Oh, I'm Floree. That's pronounced FLOW-ree, if you get my meaning. Old family name.
PRESTON. Actually, I don't get your meaning. *(Reacting to game)* OOOOHHHHHHH!!!!
FLOREE. What! What is it? Are you in pain? Did you prick your finger?
PRESTON. Did I—? No! It's the game. Didn't you hear it?
FLOREE. Game? Oh, that. I suppose. Who's playing?
PRESTON. *(Incredulous)* Who's playing?! Lady, do you know where you are?
FLOREE. Nevermind. It's not important.
PRESTON. Not important?! You have GOT to be *(reacting to flowers)* OOOOOOOOOHHHHHHHHH!!!!!!
FLOREE. What now? Did someone score a run or something?
PRESTON. *(Exasperated)* Aren't you—? Can't you—? Look at these. *(Indicates flower arrangement)* Do you see the problem now?

206

FLOREE. *(Studying the arrangement for a long time. She makes several starts and stops at offering an opinion until finally...)* No.

PRESTON. Well it should be obvious. The lily can't go next to the lilac. Too much alliteration. To many LLLLLLLLLLLLLLLs.

FLOREE. Oh really? I didn't realize that mattered when arranging flowers.

PRESTON. *(Warming to the topic)* Oh, absolutely. It's a favorite crusade of mine. Everything in life—natural and unnatural—can be broken down into how it works grammatically. It— *(the game catches his attention and he yells at the radio)* Would you come on and get off your ass for Christ's sake?!

FLOREE. *(Going to cut off the radio)* That's about enough of that.

PRESTON. Hey! What do you think you're doing there? I'm listening to the game.

FLOREE. It's not good for your health to get so worked up over a game. And it's not good for your arranging technique either. Besides. It's all just lavaloo.

PRESTON. *(Confused)* It's all just what?

FLOREE. Nevermind. We can talk about that later. Now. You were telling me about your grammatical theory.

PRESTON. What? Oh, yes. Well, it seems to me that too many people in the world are obsessed with math. People talk about math in music. Math in the solar system. Math in Nature. I wanted to give grammar its equal time.

FLOREE. You don't like math?

PRESTON. *(Bitterly)* I fucking hate math.

FLOREE. Oh, my! That's a little harsh don't you think?

PRESTON. Not at all. All those damn mathematicians. So smug. Like they're

207

better than everyone else. With their
numbers and their fractions and their
little special calculators. Ptah!

FLOREE. I see. So you've decided to focus on
(*searches for a term*) anti-math?

PRESTON. Exactly! Math is so ugly. Grammar is
beautiful. Math is basketball. Grammar is
football. Math is institutional furniture.
Grammar is a flower arrangement. It's all
so simple, don't you see?

FLOREE. Well, it's definitely all very . . .
lavaloo.

PRESTON. There's that word again. What's that?
Lavaloo?

FLOREE. Hmmmmmmm . . . let's just say that it's
my little personal crusade.

PRESTON. That's not enough. You've got to give
me more than that. What does lavaloo mean?

FLOREE. Lavaloo is . . . passion. Lavaloo is
indifference. Lavaloo is nothing important
and everything vital. It's forceful and
delicate and demanding and pleading. It
gets you out of bed in the morning and
sends you to the sheets at night. Most of
all . . . lavaloo is rage against
impotence.

PRESTON. (*Misunderstanding*) Now listen here,
lady, I don't have any problems down
there, if you know what I mean. It may
have been awhile, but this ol' flag still
flaps in the breeze.

FLOREE. (*Disappointed in him*) I should have
known. No, Preston, it has nothing to do
with your "flag." Although I suppose it
could. I'll have to think on that. In any
case, let me come at this another way.
Have you ever had tragedy in your life?

PRESTON. Well, yeah. Hasn't everyone?

FLOREE. What?

PRESTON. (*Suddenly uncomfortable*)
My—uh—wife died.

208

FLOREE. Exactly! Now how did you feel?

PRESTON. What the hell kind of question is that?! I was pissed. I was hurt. I was guilty. I was depressed. I was...

FLOREE. And what did you do?

PRESTON. Do? I cried. I beat things. I drank. I took pills. I went on a trip. I quit my job. I slept around.

FLOREE. And did any of it help?

PRESTON. (After a moment) No.

FLOREE. Did any of it bring her back? Did any of it change your feelings?

PRESTON. No.

FLOREE. (Indicating radio) And when your football team wins—does it matter? Does anything change?

PRESTON. Well, it sucks when they lose. If they don't win enough then they don't get to go to a bowl and then they don't get on TV enough and then the high school kids don't get to see them enough and then it makes recruiting more difficult an—

FLOREE. Yes, yes, yes. But does any of that Matter? With a capital "M."

PRESTON. I suppose not.

FLOREE. (Indicating flowers) Your arrangements. Do they matter?

PRESTON. With a capital "M?"

FLOREE. Yes.

PRESTON. No. No they don't.

FLOREE. There, you see. That's lavaloo.

PRESTON. So, lavaloo is everything and nothing at the same time ... but ultimately doesn't matter?

FLOREE. Well done!

PRESTON. So, nothing then really matters. Whether it's alliteration in flower arrangements or the onomatopoeia of a football game, nothing matters. There's no point. (Growing more despondent) Then I was right. Why bother? (Throwing the

209

flowers one by one) Useless! Formless!
Worthless! Hopeless!

FLOREE. *(Stopping him. Soothing, yet sternly)*
No, no, no, no, you're missing the point.
Lavaloo is freedom! Once you recognize that
all of these things ultimately can't change
the world, then you understand that you
don't have to *try* to change the world. You
can be free of that responsibility! Then
you can be free to *live*! But if you don't
understand lavaloo. If you give into the
"real" world's attempts to calm you,
control you, and pigeonhole you, then
freedom isn't possible. Don't you see? Your
wife's death, your football game, your
flowers, your grammatical crusade are all
important and unimportant at the same time.
They are important to *you* as a part of your
life and existence, but you cannot be held
responsible for making everyone else see
and appreciate your life and existence. You
are only responsible to you. "This above
all—to thine ownself be true."

PRESTON. "And it must follow as the night the
day that thou canst not then be false to
any man."

FLOREE. *(Pleased)* You know it!

PRESTON. It's *Hamlet*; everyone knows it

FLOREE. Shakespeare understood lavaloo. If
only Polonius had, he wouldn't have hidden
behind the arras and been killed. The lack
of lavaloo literally lost him his life.

PRESTON. Hey, nice alliteration!

FLOREE. Thank you, I try.

PRESTON. So, you're saying that I should focus
on myself. I should seek to make myself
happy and live up to my own standards.
That's what you mean by lavaloo.

FLOREE. That, and it's fun to yell.

PRESTON. What?

FLOREE. Go on. Try it. LAVALOOOOOOOOOO!!!!!

PRESTON. You're crazy.

(She merely looks at him. Perhaps she raises an eyebrow)

OK. Point taken. But still—

FLOREE. Go ahead. Try it. You should really like it. It's alliterative and onomatopoetic.

PRESTON. *(Weakly)* Lavaloo.

FLOREE. Wimp!

PRESTON. *(A little better)* Lavalooo!

FLOREE. Getting there.

PRESTON. *(Roaring)* LAVALOOOOOOOOOOOOO!!!!!!!!!!

FLOREE. There, now. Feel better?

PRESTON. I do. I do! LAVALOOOOOOOOOOOOO!!!!!!!!!!

FLOREE. *(Laughing)* Brilliant! Now, don't you feel ready to resume your life without the pills and the cotton-encased existence you've been getting here?

PRESTON. I think I am. I am.

FLOREE. Can you make it without all of the prescriptions and the sessions?

PRESTON. I think I can. I can.

FLOREE. Lavaloo is a talisman. To be brought out and brandished against the darkness of society, of fear, of disenchantment. It's your empowering "Yawp."

PRESTON. Walt Whitman.

FLOREE. Very good.

PRESTON. Thank you. Thank you, doctor. This is the best I've felt in a long time. The best since before Tammy died.

FLOREE. You're more than welcome. But I'm not a doctor.

PRESTON. *(Confused)* But? Who are you then? Why are you here? You came through that door. Only doctors come through that door. You're not a patient are you?

FLOREE. No. I'm not a patient.

PRESTON. You can't be a guest. No guests are allowed in these halls and I didn't know you before you came in here.

211

FLOREE. Well, let's just say that I'm not the
    typical guest, Preston.
PRESTON. *(Growing more and more agitated)* And
    how do you know my name? You called me by
    name before and I thought it was because
    you were a new doctor they sent me and you
    had looked at my chart.
*(The door opens and the White-Coated Attendant
comes in, carrying a tray of pill cups.)*
WCA. Hey, Preston. Did you hear the end of
    that game? Man, that was something! C'mon,
    time for the evening happy pills.
PRESTON. Who are you?!?
WCA. C'mon Preston, don't start that. You know
    me. I'm your pal. I'm the one who brings
    you the flowers and the radio . . . and the
    pills.
*(Preston desperately looks from one to the
other.)*

PRESTON. He can't see you. What's going on?
    WHO ARE YOU?
WCA. Uh oh. So it's like that? Are you going
    to calm down yourself, or are you going to
    make me do it.?
PRESTON. Wait a minute . . . wait a minute. How
    did you get in here? How did you know
    my name?
WCA. Preston, I come in here every day. Now
    let's do this the easy way, huh?
FLOREE. I've always been with you. I've always
    known your name. Just like you've always
    been with me. And if you look hard enough
    inside, you'll know you've always known
    my name.
PRESTON. This is bullshit. Fucking bullshit!
    Lavaloo my ass!
WCA. *(Putting down pill tray and advancing on
    Preston)* Just take it easy, man. Ain't no
    bullshit and no one wants to lather up
    your ass. Let's just calm down. Hey.

We'll talk about the game. What'd you
think of that call on the goal line?

PRESTON. *(To WCA)* Shut the fuck up. Stay out
of this. *(To Floree)* So what was all of
this about, huh? What are you? What did
all of this shit mean?

FLOREE. It means what you want it to mean,
Preston. It's lavaloo. Believe in it.
Believe in yourself. Believe in
Shakespeare. "To thine ownself be true."
*(WCA is advancing on Preston from behind
and is about to grab him)* Fight it,
Preston. Fight them. Fight him. Don't give
in to the numbness and the sameness.
Lavaloo, Preston, lavaloo!

*(WCA grabs Preston from behind. Preston wheels
on him. A furious struggle ensues)*

PRESTON. GET THE FUCK OFF ME, MAN!

WCA. CALM DOWN! JUST CALM DOWN!

FLOREE. *(Giggling and cheering him on)*
Lavalooooo, Preston, Lavaloooooo!!!!!

PRESTON. I've got it! I get it! LAVALOOOOO
OOOOOOOOOOOOOOOOOOOO!!!!!!!!!!!!!!!!!!!!!!!!!!!

FLOREE. That's right, Preston, that's right.

*(As the struggle comes to its inevitable
conclusion, Floree slips out of the door.)*

PRESTON. LAVALOOOOOOOOOOOOOOOOOOOOOOOOOOOOOO!!!!!
!!!!!!!!!!!!!!!!!!!!!!!!!!

*(Preston snaps the attendant's neck and they
both slump to the floor. A moment of silence.
Preston crawls forward)*

PRESTON. *(Panting)* I did it. I did it!
Lavalooo, Floree, Lavaloooooooo!!!!!!! *(He
looks around in vain for her)* Floree?
Floree??!! *(He looks at the attendant's
body on the floor and slowly collapses
down next to it)* Lavaloo? Lavaloo?
LAVALOOOOO!!!

(Lights out.)

213

Appendix B

FRONT PORCH REQUIEM

Paul B. Crook

Front Porch Requiem

Characters

Oparee   Elderly Southern woman—but not a "belle." She is a woman who has worked hard all of her life and is somewhat beaten down. Still, she has a wonderfully sharp tongue and wit, and relentlessly plods on doing what she feels is right.

Estelle   Another elderly Southern woman—more of a "belle" than Oparee, but she has had to work in life also. She is more vivacious than Oparee, and takes the castigations of her friend with the proverbial grain of salt—most of the time.

Setting

The front porch of a small Alabama town. August. Hot, humid, and miserable. If the porch is represented fully, it should not be the porch of a mansion, nor should it be the porch of a shack, but that of a simple, working farmhouse. A porch swing is on the stage-right side of the porch, and two rocking chairs with a table between are on the stage-left side. The front door is in the middle of the porch.

At rise, it is late afternoon of a hot August day in a small town in Alabama. We see Oparee sitting in a rocking chair SL. She has a bowl in her lap and a bowl on the table next to her. She is snapping beans in the bowl in her lap, and using the second bowl to discard stems and such.

Estelle enters from front door with two glasses of iced tea. She sits in the rocking chair next to Oparee and takes the bowl of beans from her.

> ESTELLE. Here, let me do that for you. You know you don't need to be snapping those beans with your fingers all swollen.

OPAREE. *(Snatching bowl back from her)* You give that back to me Estelle Morgan. My fingers are just fine, thank you very much. Besides, you don't snap 'em right.

ESTELLE. What d'you mean I don't snap 'em right?! I have been snapping beans just as long as you have and I think I know very well what I'm doing.

OPAREE. You do not. You always snap 'em too small. Then when I try to eat them they split and fall off my fork. I have to eat them with a spoon.

ESTELLE. Well, if you wouldn't cook them so long then they wouldn't fall apart, now would they, Miss Boil-Everything-to-Death?

OPAREE. *(glares at her and then continues to snap beans ferociously, muttering under her breath)* Your blueberry cobbler's too damn soft and your pot roast is stringy ... so don't talk to me about over-cooking beans you...

ESTELLE. *(Sweetly, knowing she has won the point)* What's that, shug? I can't hear you.

OPAREE. Nothin'

(A long silence ensues, punctuated only by the sound of beans snapping and tea being drunk)

What are you doin' over here anyway? I thought Luther and Sunny were comin' in to town tonight.

ESTELLE. *(With regret, but she's used to it by now)* Luther called and said that he had a late meeting tonight and then Ronnie has a little league game tomorrow morning. He said they'd try to make it down for Labor Day. It works out better for me anyway; I haven't had a chance to clean the house.

OPAREE. Who are you trying to fool? You keep that house so clean you'd think the Mayor's wife was coming over to inspect it every day.

215

ESTELLE. I do not—well what if I do? It's not
a crime to live in a clean house.

OPAREE. Bah!

ESTELLE. It wouldn't hurt you to give your
house a once-over every now and again,
you know.

OPAREE. Now you listen here—!

ESTELLE. *(holding up hands)* Alright, alright.

OPAREE. *(Muttering under breath again and
snapping ferociously)* Come over here and
criticize my beans and my house and—
(Out loud, now) Nothin' I do is up to your
standards is it? Hasn't been since we were
kids and you tried to correct my spelling
on that essay for ol' Mrs. Coomer ...
just because you won the damn spelling bee
and I came in second. You've always
thought you were better than me ...

ESTELLE. *(Clearly enjoying this)* Now I never
said any such thing. And I can't help it
if you couldn't spell "photosynthesis."
Any fool knows it doesn't start with
an "f."

OPAREE. Fine! Fine! Just nail me to a cross in
the front yard for all the neighborhood
to mock!

ESTELLE. *(Trying unsuccessfully to hide her
laughter as she takes Oparee's glass and
goes back inside for more tea, leaving
Oparee muttering and snapping until she
comes back with refilled glasses.)*

OPAREE. *(Finally calming down as Estelle hands
her the fresh tea)* Estelle, why are you
really here? Even if Luther and Sunny
aren't coming down tonight I still
would've expected you to be getting ready
for the First Town Days Festival. Aren't
you on the decorations committee?

ESTELLE. You know I am. But that trashy
Marjorie Cummings is on it too and she
thinks the theme this year ought to be

"Trashy Trailer Park Sluts" or something
of the kind.

OPAREE. What?!

ESTELLE. Well, not really, of course, but it
may as well be the same thing. She said at
the meeting last week that she thinks this
year we ought to highlight our "local
specialty."

OPAREE. What? Pork rinds?

ESTELLE. YES! She wants to have pork rinds on
every corner and featured in every
restaurant. She wants to have the children
from the First Baptist VBS dress up in
little pig costumes and dance along at the
front of the parade and throw bags of pork
rinds out to everyone on the street!

OPAREE. I swanee! Ever since Melvin, Sr built
that plant out there talking that nonsense
about "revolutionizin' the snack food
market" this place hasn't been worth a
bucket of warm spit. And the SMELL!

217

ESTELLE. I know, I know. Anyhow, I told
Marjorie and Ronelle that if they were
going to go forward with that ridiculous
idea they could count me out of the
committee. Can you imagine?

OPAREE. (Finishing with beans and picking up
both bowls to go inside. We hear her voice
from inside the house.)
Well I hope you didn't tell Marjorie and
Ronelle that I'd take your place. I've got
my hands full tryin' to keep that fool
Tabitha Potter from hiring her cousin's
band to play on Friday night.

ESTELLE. (Yelling inside to her) Oh, Lord. You
don't mean that awful jug band that she
had play for Willie's wedding, do you?

OPAREE. (Coming back outside with a plate of
gingersnaps and offering it to Estelle)
The very same. She thinks they're so good.
She hasn't figured out that if they're so

good why she's the only one who ever
hires 'em.

ESTELLE. *(Taking a gingersnap and taking a
bite)* Well, you certainly have your hands
full there. Remember she was able to
convince Brother Little to let them play
during the Easter Parade last year.
(Beginning to laugh)

OPAREE. *(Joining her in laughter)* Brother
Little sure did find out where they get
all there jugs from. They were so tight
they sang "Will the *scrotum* be unbroken!"
*(Both double over in laughter at the
recollection of this)*

ESTELLE. *(Catching her breath and reaching for
another gingersnap)* Your beans may be
over-cooked, but you do make the best
gingersnaps in the county.

OPAREE. Why thank you ma'am *(taking another
one herself)*. I'm inclined to agree
with you.
*(A long silence ensues, in which Estelle
begins to fidget)*
Estelle, what's wrong?

ESTELLE. Nothing!

OPAREE. Bull. You've been scurrying around for
the past two days like a young'un who
thinks he's been caught looking at the
fuzzy channels on TV. What's the matter
with you?

ESTELLE. *(Looking away—almost inaudible)*
Cancer.

OPAREE. What? Who? *(It dawns on her.)* Oh,
Estelle. When?

ESTELLE. Last month. I went in for my yearly
and Dr Frowter saw something he didn't
like. He said my right ovary looks like
it's almost gone, it's so covered with
tumors.

OPAREE. *(Bluffly)* Well, there's your answer!
He's too damn young to know what he's

218

talkin' about. He probably doesn't even
know what an ovary does.

ESTELLE. *(Quietly)* No.

OPAREE. That settles it then. Tomorrow I'm
takin' you up to UAB and we'll get that Dr
Martinez I was reading about in *Ladies'
Home Journal* last month to look at you.

ESTELLE. I alread—

OPAREE. *(unnaturally energized)* Did I tell you
that the article said that even though he
grew up poor in Venezuela he overcame his
poor heritage and made his way to the
United States where he could work as a
bean-picker or some such thing and put
himself through college and medical school
even though he had dark skin and couldn't
speak English very well and some fools
thought that made him a bad person, as if
they had any idea what kind of man he was
and now he's shown them since he's the
most successful specialist in all of the
Southeast and he has brought his poor
mother over here and built her a big ol'
house in Mountain Brook and ... *(running
out of steam)*

ESTELLE. I've already been.

OPAREE. What?

ESTELLE. I said I've already been to see your
famous Dr Martinez.

OPAREE. When?

ESTELLE. Last Wednesday.

OPAREE. You couldn't have gone last Wednesday.
That was the day you went up to Birmingham
to the Galleria to get ...
(It dawns on her.) Oh.

ESTELLE. Yes.

OPAREE. What did he say, then?

ESTELLE. Nothing. He said they had to run the
tests and should have the results this
week. Today. His office is supposed to
call me.

219

OPAREE. Well what are you doing over here
then? You ought to be home waiting for the
call. C'mon, let's go over there right—
*(She stops as Estelle holds up her cell
phone)*
Oh. I see.
(Pause.)
ESTELLE. I'm scared, Oparee.
OPAREE. *(Quietly)* I know it. I am too.
ESTELLE. *(Reviving a bit)* You are? It seems to
me that I'm the one who has reason to be
scared, not you.
OPAREE. Of course you are! But I have a right
too. What's going to happen to me if
you're not here. Why shouldn't I be scared
at losing the only friend I have left?
Don't I have a right to be scared too?
ESTELLE. *(Soothing her)* Yes, 'Ree, you do.
I know.
OPAREE. Have you told Luther yet?
ESTELLE. No! And don't you say anything
either. I don't want to worry him.
OPAREE. Well that's probably a good idea. No
need to tell anyone anything until you
hear back about those tests. Which I just
know are gonna say that there is
absolutely nothing wrong with you. And if
not, then we'll drive to Atlanta tomorrow.
My niece Sarah's husband works at Piedmont
Hospital and I bet they have someone who
can see you there.
ESTELLE. I am not letting you drive me all the
way to Atlanta tomorrow. Anyway, Sarah's
husband works in the damn cafeteria! How
is that going to help me see a doctor?
Besides, you've got your own things to do
what with the jug band fiasco and all.
OPAREE. Nonsense! Tabitha can bring in all her
relatives and they can play combs and saws
for all I care. I am driving you to
Atlanta.

220

ESTELLE. I don't want you to—

OPAREE. I said "nonsense." I am driving you
and that's that.

ESTELLE. Let's just wait and see what Dr
Martinez's office says.

OPAREE. Hmmmm.

(*Oparee goes into the house and returns
with two brown grocery sacks full of corn.
She goes back to retrieve two plastic
trash cans to put the shucks in, with the
shucked ears going back into the sacks.*)

OPAREE. Well, when are they supposed to call?

ESTELLE. I don't know, 'Ree. They just said it
would be sometime today. Believe it or
not, you are not the only one who is
anxious about this.

OPAREE. Oh, I know you're anxious too. Who
wouldn't be? I wonder why it's taken them
a whole week to get the results.

ESTELLE. He didn't say. He just said they had
to send the test off to Houston. They'd be
able to check it better at that place.

OPAREE. Hmph! Texas. Just because they have a
big state and just because they have all
of them millionaires they keep thinking
they're better than all the rest of us. I
don't see what's so special about Texas
that they can do better than UAB. It's
just ridiculous!

ESTELLE. Would you shut up about Texas?! We
all know you haven't liked the entire
state ever since that Wainwright boy moved
into town from Abilene and then broke your
heart because he only went out with you
once and then started goin' with Mary
Simon Gallahan . . . and then married her!

OPAREE. You shut up.

ESTELLE. (*Clearly enjoying the memory*) He said
he couldn't go out with you anymore 'cause
you bit his tongue when he kissed you!
(*Shaking with laughter*)

221

OPAREE. You had best stop it this minute
Estelle.

*(Estelle explodes with laughter. After a
moment, Oparee begins to join her.)*

Well, it wasn't my fault. Nobody'd ever
done that to me before. Hell, I'd never
been kissed before. I thought maybe he
was choking or something and his tongue
was just pushed in there by accident. I
was so surprised I couldn't help but
bite down!

ESTELLE. *(Settling down a bit)* Ahhhhhh . . . he
was cute, though.

OPAREE. I suppose.

ESTELLE. It's just as well you did bite him.
You know how much he ran around on Mary
Simon after they were married.

OPAREE. Well I can't say I was surprised. Her
cornbread has always been crumbly.

ESTELLE. Mmm-hmm.

OPAREE. *(Solemnly)* You know what they say:
"Crumbly cornbread—bumbling in bed."

ESTELLE. WHAT?

OPAREE. You heard me.

ESTELLE. Who says that? No one says that. You
just made that up.

OPAREE. *(Beginning to giggle)* Well maybe I
did. But I bet it's true.

ESTELLE. *(Throwing a shuck at her)* You're
terrible.

OPAREE. Maybe. But I made you smile. It's the
first real one I've seen today.

ESTELLE. *(pause)* I know.

OPAREE. *(pause)* What're you going to do? If
it's . . .

ESTELLE. I don't know.

OPAREE. Are you going to tell Luther?

ESTELLE. Not yet.

OPAREE. Then when?

ESTELLE. I don't know! Not yet.

OPAREE. You want me to tell him?

ESTELLE. *(sighing)* No. I will. Just—not yet. OK?

OPAREE. OK then.

    (Finishes with her corn and picks up her sack, moving to Estelle and sitting on the swing next to her.)

ESTELLE. It's strange, you know?

OPAREE. What's that?

ESTELLE. I always thought something like this would frighten me. But it doesn't. Don't get me wrong—I'm scared, but I'm not *frightened*. I don't know what the results of the test are going to be and at times I'm not sure I want to know. But I do know that whatever they are, it's alright. If it's time, it's time. I've been fortunate with everything *(looks at Oparee)*—especially with you.

OPAREE. *(Swatting her)* Now you just stop that.

ESTELLE. Well it's true!

OPAREE. I don't care how true it is. You just stop it right now. I refuse to believe that anything will be wrong. And even if there is, then that cute Dr Martinez will be able to handle it, I'm sure. And if not, there's always Atlanta.

ESTELLE. *(Grabbing Oparee's hand)* You keep thinking that then . . . and we'll just see what happens.

OPAREE. *(Letting forth a big sigh)* Yes we will, won't we?

    (As lights fade, Estelle's cell phone begins to ring.)

223

Glossary of Terms

Throughout the book, you may have run across words and terms that are unfamiliar to you. While you may know the definition of the words, perhaps you have not encountered them the way they are used here. This glossary should help you with any terminology that is new for you. While terms may differ from company to company, these are all fairly common usages.

AAE: Action—Adjustment—Expectation. A three-column method of blocking notation that focuses on where the actor moves, how the actor adjusts, and why.

Activation: The process of an actor breathing life into and fleshing out a character.

Actor-manager: A pre-twentieth-century term for an actor who also served as the de facto general manager of a theatre company.

AEA ("Equity"): Actors' Equity Association. The professional union for actors and stage managers.

Arc: The growth and development of a character from the beginning of a show to the end.

Archeology: An improv game in which actors provide the archaeological "history" of an everyday object.

Arena (staging): A type of staging in which the audience surrounds the performance space. Also called "theatre in the round."

Blocking: The process of moving the actors around the stage at a determined and specific moment in a production.

Callback: A secondary audition when directors call certain actors back after the primary audition, in order to see more of their work.

Callboard: A physical bulletin board where information about auditions, rehearsals, calls, and job opportunities can be posted. See also "virtual callboard."

Cattle-call: Auditions that are open to a wide group of actors, and typically involve hundreds of auditionees. Those auditioning are given a brief, specified time to perform some combination of monologues and songs.

Central image: The distillation of a script into a single image. The central image is typically a metaphorical representation of the idea of the show.

Cold read: A type of audition where the actors are given a portion of the script to read with limited preparation.

Collaboration: The process of working with other artists to bring a show to life.

Colorblind casting: Casting that ignores an actor's race, ethnicity, or skin color, and instead focuses solely on which actor can best play the role.

Color-conscious casting: Casting that specifically considers utilizing under-represented actors of color for roles they might not be otherwise considered for in "mainstream" casting.

Comp(s): Short for "complimentary." A ticket (or tickets) provided free of charge to a patron (or patrons).

Consumables: Stage props that will be used up with each performance (i.e. food, liquid, cigarettes, etc.).

Costume parade: The first opportunity for actors to wear their costumes onstage, so that the director and designers can evaluate the look and execution of the design. See also: "dress parade."

Costume plot: A document that indicates what costume pieces actors are to wear in each scene.

Definite tech: A technical rehearsal with an established and agreed-upon, specific date.

Design meeting: A meeting with all of the designers of a production, usually also attended by stage management and crew heads. Design meetings can take place before production begins, but also during the course of rehearsals.

Dramatic action: The action of a script that is central to the plot and tells the story of the play.

Dramatic function: The purpose of a given character or scene in a play. The reason the playwright has included the character or scene.

Dramaturgy(-ical): The study of dramatic composition, including research, historical, and production information.

Dress parade: The first opportunity for actors to wear their costumes onstage, so the director and designers can evaluate the look and execution of the design. See also: "costume parade."

Dress rehearsal: A rehearsal in which the actors are all wearing the (mostly) finished costumes. Dress rehearsals come at the end of the rehearsal process, immediately prior to opening.

225

Ethereal design concepts: Design elements, like lighting and sound, that do not have a tactile representation (i.e. scenic, props, or costumes).

Fight director: The person responsible for all stage combat in a production. Though not required, this person is often certified through a governing body, such as the Society of American Fight Directors (SAFD).

Final dress: The last rehearsal before opening, when the show is typically run under "performance conditions."

Freeze frame: An improv game in which participants begin performing an improvised scene, only to be told to freeze, allowing another actor to step into the scene and change its given circumstances.

French scene: An organizational division of a script based on the entrances and exits of principal characters.

Given circumstances: The information provided by the playwright that establishes the status quo of the play.

Gradual tech: A method of technical rehearsal that does not rely on a single, established date, but instead inserts technical elements into the show over a period of time.

Guerrilla theatre: An informal term referring to shows produced on no budget and in a variety of locations: storefronts, parks, bars, etc.

Inciting incident: The moment in the play that kicks off the action of the story.

Liturgical drama: Plays with religious themes and/or tropes, often produced by a church or other religious institution (e.g. Passion Plays produced at Easter).

LORT: League of Resident Theatres. A professional theatre organization that oversees and administers contracts for not-for-profit theatres across the country.

Matrix: A tool used by directors in script analysis. Matrix deals with the "world of" the playwright, the play, etc.

Meiningen Players (also Ensemble and Company): The court theatre company under the direction of Georg II, Duke of Saxe-Meiningen, that was active in Germany and Europe from 1874–1890. Credited with establishing one of the first modern ensemble companies, and creating the Duke as the first modern director.

Movement chart: A blocking notation method that utilizes a groundplan of the set and arrows depicting the movement of actors.

226

Non-traditional casting: Casting, often conceptual, that goes against the "standard" type of actor considered for a role or role (e.g. casting a woman in the role of Hamlet).

Objective: A character-analysis term for actors (and directors) that refers to a character's goal or desire.

Obstacle: A character-analysis term for actors (and directors) that refers to what (or who) is in the way of a character reaching her or his objective.

Off-book: The process, by actors, of working without a script, having memorized their lines.

Paper tech: A rehearsal typically including stage management and designers (and occasionally board ops), involving going through the script to ensure that all of the warnings and cues are in the correct spot in the script.

Pick-up rehearsal: A run-through rehearsal held after the play has been open, but having had a break in the run.

Plot: The framework of the story, the "skeleton" of the play.

Post-mortem: A process of evaluating the relative success of a production after its run has concluded.

Practical (scenery, props, etc.): A scenic, lighting, or property element (such as a lamp, stove, radio, etc.) that is meant to function on stage in the course of a production.

Pre-blocking: The process of notating blocking in a script prior to rehearsals beginning.

Primary action: The main action of a scene or play for a character or characters. The primary action typically determines the character's arc.

Production meeting: A meeting of all production and technical crew members to discuss details surrounding the production.

Production team: The creative and artistic heads of a production, usually including the director, production stage manager, designers, and artistic director. Includes choreographer, fight director, music director, assistant directors, and vocal coach where appropriate.

Promenade (staging): A type of staging with no defined locations for the stage or audience.

Proscenium (staging): A type of staging on a traditional "picture-frame" stage, with the audience positioned in front of the stage, to look in through the "fourth wall."

PSM: Production stage manager. The stage manager in charge of a production.

Psychological gesture: An acting term associated with Michael Chekhov's technique, dealing with an archetypical gesture that begins externally and is then internalized.

Put-in rehearsal: A rehearsal, typically held during the run of the show, for the purpose of preparing understudies or replacement actors.

Q2Q (also "cue to cue"): A technical rehearsal that skips from one technical cue to another.

Read-through: A rehearsal that involves the actors sitting and reading through the script, often for the first time.

Reader: A person (sometimes an actor, sometimes a production assistant) hired to read scenes with actors during an audition.

Renderings: Color drawings typically made by scenic and costume designers of their finished designs.

Run-through: A rehearsal in which the actors perform the entire show, usually without stopping and often with few, if any, technical elements.

Snapshot moment: A moment of staging in which the positioning of the actors, combined with the design elements, stands out as "photographic" in the memory of the audience.

Speed-through: A rehearsal in which the actors go through their lines (with or without blocking) at double the usual pace. Also called an "Italian run-through."

Status: The level of importance held by characters onstage in a given scene.

Story: Specifically, the events that make up the action of the play; the "muscles, ligaments, tendons, and skin" of a script.

Structure: The way in which a playwright organizes a script.

Super objective: A character analysis term for actors (and directors) that refers to a character's overall goal or desire.

Table work: Rehearsal work, typically taking place with the actors seated around a table, that can include read-throughs, character study, dialect work, dramaturgical, or other show-specific work for the actors.

Target audience: The primary audience for whom a production (or productions) is meant.

Tech rehearsal: A rehearsal where the primary purpose is for the installation and perfection of all technical elements.

Tech-dress: A technical rehearsal in which the actors may be wearing some (or even all) costume pieces, but the primary focus is still on the technical elements.

Thrust (staging): A type of staging in which the audience is positioned around three sides of the stage.

Tudor (poetry): Poetry written during the Tudor period in England (1485–1603), including work by Thomas Wyatt, the Earl of Surrey, Philip Sidney, Edmund Spenser, and William Shakespeare.

Unified auditions: Auditions held with representatives of multiple theatre companies in attendance, all looking to cast for their seasons.

Unit: A script-analysis term that designates a section of a script that contains a single or connected group of thoughts.

Virtual callboard: An electronic or online bulletin/message board, where information about auditions, rehearsals, calls, and job opportunities can be posted. See also "callboard."

Vocal coach: A member of the production team whose responsibility is to work with actors on vocal production necessary for the show.

Wings: The backstage area immediately on either side of the stage.

Index

Page numbers in **bold** denote figures.

Wilson, Lanford, *The Hot l Baltimore* 16–17
working rehearsals 145, 155; off-book rehearsals 103, 149–50; on-book rehearsals 145–8

W;t (Edson) **135**, 135–6

Z
Zorro! (Richmond) 132, **132**

235